SCIENTIFIC ARTICLE WRITING (SAW) 101

A Complete Guide For Students To Scientific Writing With Academic Supervisor

Wan Mohd Aizat, PhD

Copyright © 2024 Wan Mohd Aizat

All rights reserved.

ISBN: 9798322086543

Table of Content

Table of Content 4

List of figures 9

List of tables 21

Preface 24

Chapter 1 Introduction 30

Chapter 2 The History Of Peer Review And Its Recent Process 38
    The history 38
    Recent process of peer review 41

Chapter 3 Roles, Challenges And Expectations Of Students And Supervisors During Scientific Writing 48

Roles of students and supervisors 48

Challenges during the publication process 54

Managing expectation 60

Chapter 4 The 10 Steps Of Successful Writing With Your Supervisors 68

Step 1 70

Step 2 73

Step 3 77

Step 4 79

Step 5 81

Step 6 84

Step 7 86

Step 8 88

Step 9 93

Step 10 95

Chapter 5 Strategy To Write A Research Manuscript 101

Manuscript types 102

Understanding journal impact factor and quartile 109

Research manuscript arrangement 114

Methods section: the toolbox 117

Results section: the descriptor 119

Introduction section: the prelude 121

Discussion section: the deliberation *124*
Conclusion: the endgame *126*
Abstract: the summation *128*
Title: the attraction *130*
References: the sources *132*

Chapter 6 Strategy To Write A Review Manuscript **137**
Exploring the Pros and Cons of Review Papers *137*
Systematic review *141*
Scoping review *151*
Traditional review *153*
Review manuscript arrangement *159*
A systematic literature search *161*

Chapter 7 Ethics in publications **182**
Authorship *182*
Plagiarism *200*
Copyright *201*
Fabrication *207*
Predatory publication *211*

Chapter 8 How to mitigate problems in writing? **217**
Find help *217*
Social network and online pages *219*
Conclusion *223*

References **226**

Index **232**

About the Author **235**

List of figures

Figure 1.1 The process of writing a scientific manuscript and getting it published can be a lengthy and difficult journey.......... 31

Figure 1.2 Distribution of papers based on the number of weeks taken for the first decision in Angewandte Chemie International Edition Journal. The depicted percentages vary from a very short reviewing period (< 3 weeks) to an extensively protracted process (21-60 weeks). The figure incorporates data from Bornmann and Daniel (2010), remaining valid until its publication date only.. 33

Figure 1.3 One of the longest manuscript review periods on record. This paper (Aslaksen and Sletsjøe 2009) was submitted on the 14th of June 1995 and only accepted after nearly 11 years on the 8th of May 2006. The full article was then officially published in 2009 and can be viewed from this link: https://doi.org/10.1016/j.laa.2006.05.022. Permission to reuse article excerpt is obtained from Elsevier under license number 5751151233114. 34

Figure 2.1 The history of manuscript peer review, as described by Spier (2002). 39

Figure 2.2 The end phase of publishing scientific manuscripts involves the editor, who plays a pivotal role (hence the crown depicted in the figure) in making decisions regarding submitted manuscripts. 43

Figure 2.3 The writing phase of a scientific publication. The main supervisor plays a crucial role in determining the fate of the manuscript. 46

Figure 4.1 The 10 steps for successful publication with your supervisors. 69

Figure 4.2 The primary stride towards achieving a successful publication involves initiating a discussion with the supervisor regarding the specifics of figures and tables prior to embarking on the actual writing process. 71

Figure 4.3 The second step in the journey towards successful writing entails commencing the first draft with a well-thought-out plan and the requisite skills. 76

Figure 4.4 Step 3 entails the submission of your initial draft to the principal supervisor. 78

Figure 4.5 Step 4 involves the crucial process of managing feedback from your supervisor. 80

Figure 4.6 In Step 5, the finalization of the draft is achieved by revisiting and repeating the processes outlined in the earlier Steps 3 and 4. 82

Figure 4.7 In Step 6, the manuscript is submitted to all co-authors for their thorough review and input. 85

Figure 4.8 Step 7 underscores the importance of managing feedback from co-authors. 87

Figure 4.9 In Step 8, proofreading takes center stage, addressing either similarity checks or language refinement. 89

Figure 4.10 In Step 9, the focus is on the meticulous preparation of documents in accordance with the specific requirements of the chosen journal. 94

Figure 4.11 The final step in achieving a successful publication with your supervisor is, indeed, the submission of the manuscript to the journal of interest. 96

Figure 5.1 List of Web of Science-indexed journals from the multidisciplinary science field, indicating the journal impact factor and other metrics, such as total cites and Eigenfactor score. Only the top 10 highest-impact journals from this category are displayed (the screenshot was obtained from https://jcr.clarivate.com/ in July 2019)... 110

Figure 5.2 Enumerating Scopus-indexed journals within the multidisciplinary domain, we delineate the journal quartiles, focusing specifically on the top five journals bearing the coveted Q1 rank. Additionally, various metrics, including the H-index and SCImago Journal Rank (SJR), are presented for elucidation. It is pertinent to note that the accompanying screenshot was procured from https://www.scimagojr.com/ in July 2019. 112

Figure 5.3 Two choices of research manuscript arrangements, AIMeRDisC and AIRDCoM. 115

Figure 5.4 An example of an excellent manuscript title by Bunawan et al. (2011). Manuscript front page courtesy of Hamidun Bunawan. 131

Figure 5.5 The referencing style used by PeerJ. Such details can be obtained from the journal website (https://peerj.com/about/author-instructions/). 133

Figure 6.1 The various types of review articles include systematic, scoping, and traditional reviews. The latter, traditional reviews, can be further subdivided into synthesis and narrative reviews. 140

Figure 6.2 An example of a systematic review on childhood obesity intervention (Lacombe et al. 2019). Reproduced with permission under the Creative Commons Attribution 4.0 CC-BY license (https://doi.org/10.1186/s12889-019-7030-8). 142

Figure 6.3 The PRISMA workflow for identifying and selecting research papers to be reviewed. Reprinted from http://prisma-statement.org/ (Moher et al. 2009). 150

Figure 6.4 Prospero website for registering systematic review protocols (https://www.crd.york.ac.uk/PROSPERO/)... 151

Figure 6.5 An example of a scoping review on various measurements and indicators for maternal and newborn babies (Moller et al., 2018). Reprinted permission is granted under the Creative Commons Attribution 4.0 CC-BY license (https://doi.org/10.1371/journal.pone.0204763). 153

Figure 6.6 An example of a synthesis review regarding the benefits of Omalizumab therapy against a specific type of pulmonary infection is presented by Li et al. (2017). In this synthesis review, the main sections encompass the method of analysis and the selection of journal papers. These aspects can be narrowed down and predetermined to shape the content of the review (https://doi.org/10.1016/j.rmed.2016.11.019). Permission to reuse article excerpt is obtained from Elsevier under license number 5751731037737. 155

Figure 6.7 An example of a narrative review, which explores mangosteen applications in various studies, is presented by

Aizat et al. (2019). In this narrative review, the sections are broad, covering postharvest, food, and engineering applications of this species. Reprinted permission was obtained from Elsevier (https://doi.org/10.1016/j.jare.2019.05.005). 156

Figure 6.8 The primary subsections within review articles. 160

Figure 6.9 The eight steps for composing a review article. 162

Figure 6.10 The process for retrieving a literature list from Web of Science involves entering keywords into the search box (A), followed by the collection of a number of relevant literatures from the database (B). Subsequently, information for these articles can be downloaded (C and D) to facilitate the systematic review process. 166

Figure 6.11 The steps for retrieving a literature list from the Scopus database involve searching for keywords (A), resulting in the collection of a number of relevant literatures from the database (B). The information for these articles can then be downloaded (C and D) for use in a systematic review process. 169

Figure 6.12 Converting an excel sheet (A) into a functional table (B). 171

Figure 6.13 How to find similar entries from two different databases. A) Fuzzy lookup icon, B) Fuzzy lookup settings, C) Similar entries between two databases have similarity above 0.9. 173

Figure 6.14 The downloaded list from certain databases, such as Science Direct, requires a pre-processing step using Notepad++ and Excel. The text file downloaded must first be opened in Notepad++ (A) before spaces are removed, and "keywords" are aligned (B). Then, the list can be pasted into Excel (C) before being converted to text columns (D and E). The resulting list will consist of a data table with separating columns between the elements. 177

Figure 7.1 The guidelines of the International Committee of Medical Journal of Editors (ICJME) on authorship. Statement reprinted from http://www.icmje.org/. 184

Figure 7.2 The guidelines of the International Committee of Medical Journal Editors (ICJME) on individuals who should NOT be considered authors but can be acknowledged. Statement reprinted from http://www.icmje.org/. 185

Figure 7.3 A typical acknowledgement section from a publication (Pang et al., 2019). Reprinted with permission under the Creative Commons Attribution 4.0 CC-BY license (https://www.nature.com/articles/s41598-019-40879-x). 187

Figure 7.4 International Committee of Medical Journal Editors (ICMJE) guidelines for authorship arrangement (http://www.icmje.org/). 189

Figure 7.5 The arrangement of authors can be contingent on their contributions and seniority in the project. Nevertheless, all authors must meet the conditions stipulated by the International Committee of Medical Journal Editors (ICJME). 191

Figure 7.6 The recent news highlights problems arising from the order of authorship in a publication. The scientist faced termination for asserting her right to be the first author on a submitted paper. The complete article is available at https://www.sciencemag.org/news/2018/10/was-cancer-scientist-fired-challenging-lab-chief-over-authorship. Reproduction permission has been authorized by the publisher (Science Journals/AAAS). 192

Figure 7.7 The different labels associated with various authorship practices. 194

Figure 7.8 The author contribution statement example is drawn from Ahmad et al. (2018), typically positioned near the end of the manuscript. Reprinted permission is granted under the Creative Commons Attribution 4.0 CC-BY license (https://www.nature.com/articles/s41598-018-22485-5). 197

Figure 7.9 A declaration of competing interests can be included in articles to elucidate any external influences (if present) on the presented findings. Reprinted with permission under the Creative Commons Attribution 4.0 CC-BY license (https://journals.plos.org/plosone/article?id=10.1371/journal.pone.0167958). 198

Figure 7.10 The four types of plagiarism are as follows: direct, self, mosaic, and accidental (https://www.bowdoin.edu/dean-of-students/conduct-review-board/academic-honesty-and-plagiarism/common-types-of-plagiarism.html) 201

Figure 7.11 Obtaining permission for the use of journal materials through a publisher's website involves the following steps: A) Any journal publication website will typically have a section labeled "Get rights and content" or a similar indication for their published manuscripts (highlighted in red). B) Upon selecting this option, authors will be redirected to RightsLink, where they can officially request permission for reuse. C) Authors can then specify how they intend to use the materials. D) After providing details such as the publisher's name, intended reuse format (print or online or both), and other particulars, a price will be presented for the requested use. This fee must be paid before obtaining permission. In cases where the author of the paper is making the request, there may be no charges associated with its reuse (Quick price = 0.00 USD). Reprinted permission was obtained from Elsevier (https://doi.org/10.1016/j.scienta.2018.01.061). 203

Figure 7.12 Another pitfall in scientific writing is data fabrication—presenting falsified data to support a specific hypothesis or argument. Permission to reuse the figure has been obtained from Glasbergen Cartoon Service (http://www.glasbergen.com).. 208

Figure 7.13 The ramifications of data fabrication can have severe consequences for scientists. The left panel displays the manuscript with a retraction label (https://doi.org/10.18632/aging.102756). On the right panel, a corresponding note accompanies the retracted article, providing justification for the retraction, in this instance attributed to data fabrication (https://doi.org/10.18632/aging.205525). Reprinted with permission under the Creative Commons Attribution 3.0 and 4.0 CC-BY licenses, respectively............................ 210

Figure 7.14 A deceptive email soliciting manuscripts for publication in a journal might tempt scientists with the promise of quick and easy publishing. It is important to be aware that such journals could be predatory, driven solely by profit and lacking genuine interest in your scientific work!........... 212

Figure 7.15 The webpages for checking journals indexed by both Web of Science (A) (https://jcr.clarivate.com/JCRJournalHomeAction.action) and Scopus (B) (https://www.scimagojr.com/journalrank.php). 214

Figure 7.16 The homepage of Beall's List of Predatory Journals and Publishers can be accessed at https://beallslist.weebly.com/. 215

Figure 8.1 Several options are available for seeking help in the event of conflicts during studentship. 218

Figure 8.2 Several social media pages provide support for postgraduate students. These platforms offer advice, tips, and motivation throughout our research journey. 221

Figure 8.3 The "Piled Higher and Deeper" webcomic (www.phdcomics.com) serves as a means of escape from the stresses encountered in laboratories. Created by Jorge Cham, it provides a lighthearted perspective on the challenges faced by individuals involved in academic and research pursuits. 222

List of tables

Table 3.1 Similarities and differences between a school teacher and a lecturer/supervisor. 50

Table 3.2 The distinct roles of postgraduate students and supervisors during the manuscript write-up process. 51

Table 3.3 Writing issues from the perspectives of students and supervisors. 55

Table 3.4 Common reasons for busy schedules among supervisors and students. 58

Table 3.5 Characteristics of ideal students and supervisors from both perspectives. 61

Table 4.1 An approximate pricing overview for various English editing services from international and national (Malaysia is given as an example) companies as of April-May 2019. Please note that these prices may have changed, and it's advisable to check the respective websites for the most current information and service details. 90

Table 5.1 The various manuscript types, their attributes, and example journals (non-exhaustive) featuring them are detailed here. Predominantly situated in multidisciplinary domains, these journals ensure extensive applicability to both students and supervisors. It is pertinent to note that the specified word limits serve as approximations, given the potential divergence in guidelines among individual journals. PLoS, Public Library of Science; PNAS, Proceedings of the National Academy of Sciences of the United States of America. 103

Table 6.1 Advantages and disadvantages of a review article 138

Table 6.2 The PRISMA checklist for writing a systematic review and/or meta-analysis. Reprinted from http://prisma-statement.org/. 143

Table 6.3 The difference between systematic, scoping and traditional reviews.. 157

Table 7.1 Different copyright license types are identified by specific abbreviations, symbols, and meanings. 205

Preface

Embarking on the journey of manuscript writing, I am thrilled to present this book, a culmination of my experiences and insights gained during my academic odyssey. As a former student, now an associate professor, my passion for writing has woven seamlessly through the tapestry of my undergraduate and PhD years. This book germinated from my quest to unravel the intricacies of the student-supervisor relationship during the critical writing phase, a phase often overlooked but paramount in the pursuit of successful publications.

My journey in writing, initially marred by red marks and comments, was illuminated by the guiding light of exceptional mentors. Dr. Carolyn Schultz and Prof. Dr. Amanda J. Able, my Honours and Ph.D. supervisors respectively, patiently nurtured my writing skills. Their mentorship laid the foundation for my subsequent success in publishing four scientific articles during my higher education. This book is a tribute to their invaluable guidance and enduring patience.

Returning to my homeland, Malaysia, after completing my Ph.D. in 2013, I assumed the roles of a research fellow and senior lecturer. It was during this phase that I confronted the challenges inherent in guiding students through their writing struggles. Recognizing the scarcity of literature addressing the nuances of the student-supervisor relationship during the writing process, I endeavored to fill this void.

The genesis of this book can be traced back to my 2018 lecture, "Publishing with your Supervisor(s): Responsibilities, Challenges, and Ethics," which resonated positively with its audience. Encouraged by this response, I embarked on the ambitious task of expanding my insights into a comprehensive book called "Scientific Article Writing (SAW) 101: A Complete Guide For Students To Scientific Writing With Academic Supervisor", aimed at a global audience of students and supervisors alike. It is my sincere hope that the shared experiences, challenges, and ethical considerations explored within these pages will serve as a beacon for those navigating the intricate path of manuscript preparation and publication.

I extend heartfelt gratitude to the students and research assistants who have walked alongside me, shaping not only my academic path but also contributing unwittingly to the principles outlined in this book. Special acknowledgment is due to Othman Mazlan, Siti Farah Mamat, Azhani Abdul Rahman, Salahuddin Sanusi, Ili Nadhirah Jamil, and Juwairiah Remali, the inaugural members of my student cohort, who unknowingly became 'subjects' of the experimentation process outlined within these pages. My other students, who followed suit, including Muhammad Aqil Fitri Bin Rosli, Nur Amirah Syahirah Binti Ibrahim, Hariyani Reddy Murugiah, and many more, have also successfully undergone similar training and published various articles.

Numerous individuals have left an indelible mark on my academic journey. Prof. Dr. Normah Mohd Noor and Prof. Dr. Syarul Nataqain Baharum, played pivotal roles in my career development. Prof. Dr. Ismanizan Ismail's encouragement to write this book and his trust in leading the *Unit Bimbingan INBIOSIS* (UBI) (translated as INBIOSIS Support Unit) opened avenues for insights into student counseling and development. I extend my deepest gratitude to all the fellows and staff at INBIOSIS UKM for their remarkable contributions to shaping my research attitude and student development. I would like to also express my gratitude to Assoc. Prof. Dr. Wan Mohd Hirwani Wan Hussain for introducing me to KDP

Amazon publishing, which has been an essential tool for this book publication.

To the readers embarking on this manuscript writing journey, I extend my warmest wishes for a successful and fulfilling expedition. To tell the truth, despite being an experienced writer with more than 70 scientific articles and books published to date, I continue to face rejections from publishers and journals every now and then (though perhaps at a lesser rate compared to when I was still a novice). Even this very book here has been rejected multiple times by various publishers, yet I have never given up on publishing it. Remember, everything may seem impossible until it is accomplished!

Wan Mohd Aizat, PhD
Institute of Systems Biology (INBIOSIS)
Universiti Kebangsaan Malaysia (UKM), 43600 Bangi, Selangor, Malaysia
Grant number: GP-K019471

Chapter 1 Introduction

Scientific writing and publication may initially appear formidable to early career researchers, but with the right techniques and skills, it is certainly achievable. As illustrated in Figure 1.1, the process can indeed be extensive and demanding. It commences with designing and executing experiments, analysing data, creating figures and tables, and drafting the manuscript. Upon completing the final draft, additional steps come into play, including proofreading, selecting an appropriate journal, formatting the manuscript, submitting it, undergoing peer review, and eventually receiving a decision from the journal editor. If the manuscript secures acceptance, it proceeds to publication.

However, in the event of rejection, authors must identify a new target journal and commence the entire process anew.

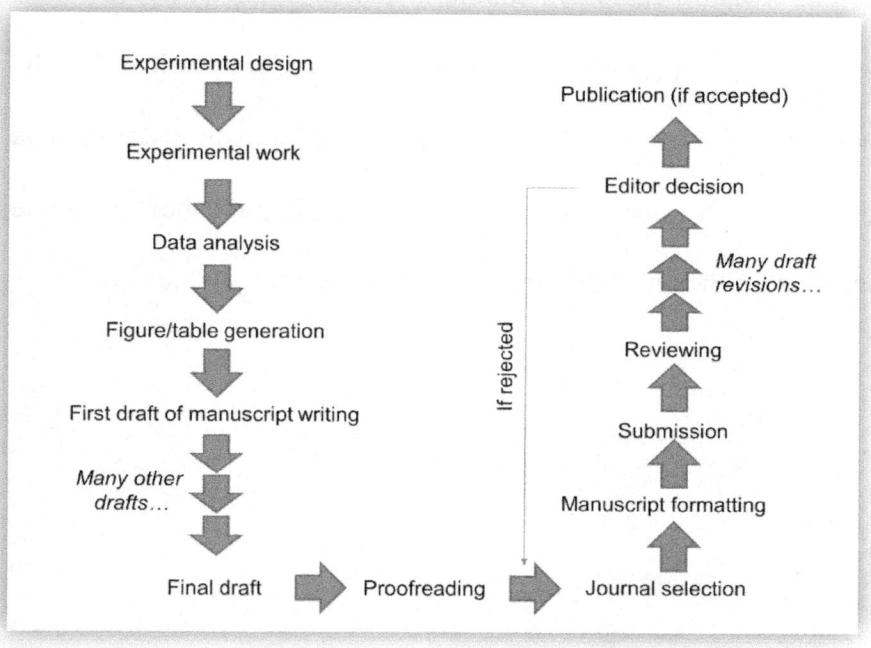

Figure 1.1 The process of writing a scientific manuscript and getting it published can be a lengthy and difficult journey.

The scientific peer review process serves as a mechanism to validate the credibility of the reported work. Although it is time-consuming, the feedback provided by reviewers can significantly improve the clarity and scientific rigour of a paper, thereby enhancing its overall quality. Few papers are accepted without some degree of revision or modification. In certain instances, the required revisions are extensive, necessitating additional experimentation in the laboratory. For example, Angewandte Chemie International Edition, a journal with an impact factor of 12.1 in 2017, published an article underscoring the prolonged duration of this process. (Figure 1.2).

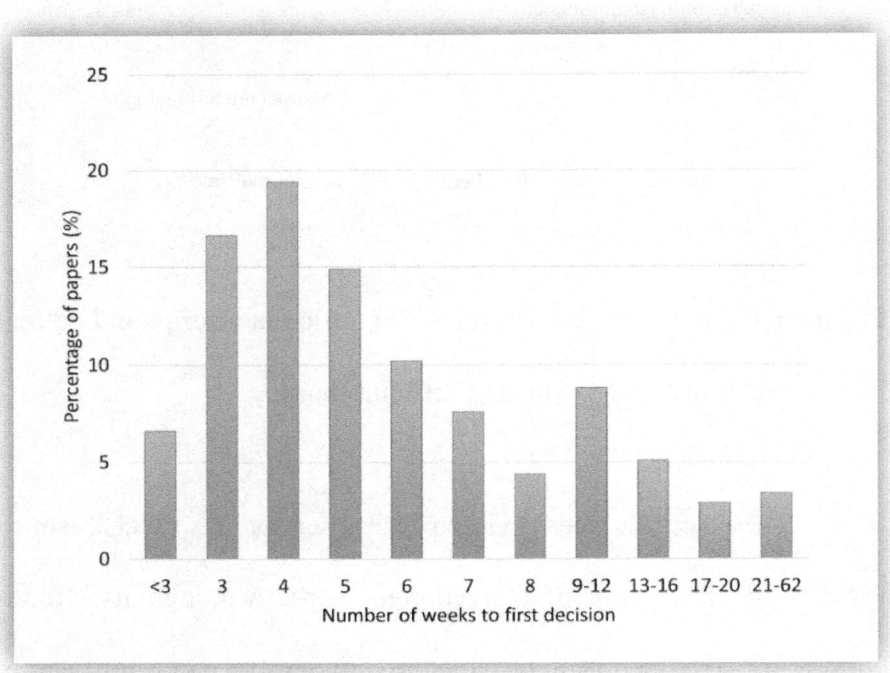

Figure 1.2 Distribution of papers based on the number of weeks taken for the first decision in Angewandte Chemie International Edition Journal. The depicted percentages vary from a very short reviewing period (< 3 weeks) to an extensively protracted process (21-60 weeks). The figure incorporates data from Bornmann and Daniel (2010), remaining valid until its publication date only.

More than 50% of the submissions to the Angewandte Chemie International Edition Journal were processed within 6 weeks of submission. However, in some instances, the review process extended to 62 weeks, equivalent to a year and a half! Although such occurrences are uncommon, the path to acceptance can indeed be quite protracted, especially when manuscripts are transferred from one journal to another. Nevertheless, authors need not lose hope if they encounter this situation. Figure 1.3 illustrates the timeline for one of the lengthiest manuscripts ever reviewed and subsequently accepted. This particular paper (Aslaksen and Sletsjøe, 2009) was initially submitted on the 14th of June 1995 and received acceptance nearly 11 years later, on the 8th of May 2006. The full article was officially published in 2009 and is accessible via the following link: https://doi.org/10.1016/j.laa.2006.05.022.

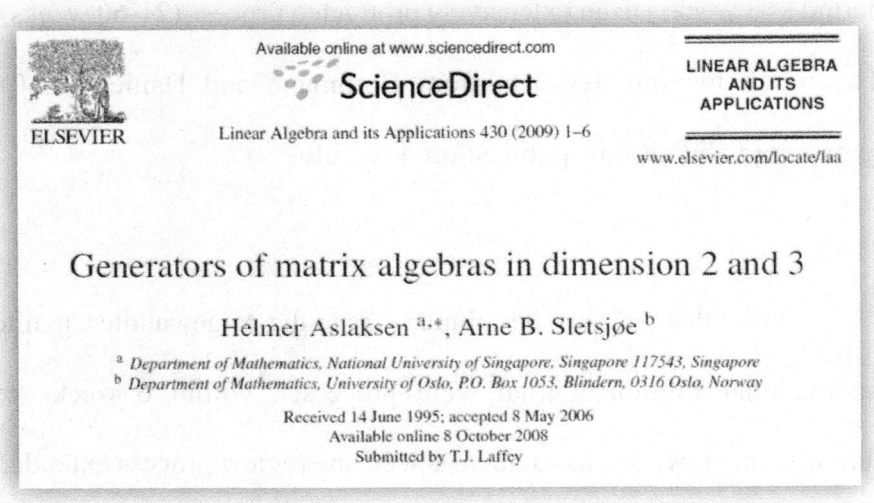

Figure 1.3 One of the longest manuscript review periods on record. This paper (Aslaksen and Sletsjøe 2009) was submitted on the 14th of June 1995 and only accepted after nearly 11 years on the 8th of May 2006. The full article was then officially published in 2009 and can be viewed from this link: https://doi.org/10.1016/j.laa.2006.05.022. Permission to reuse article excerpt is obtained from Elsevier under license number 5751151233114.

The process of peer review has endured for centuries, serving as a cornerstone of scientific integrity and ensuring the credibility of scholarly publications. Chapter 2 will explore the historical evolution of peer review and illuminate current trends in scientific publishing. This knowledge is indispensable for aspiring authors, particularly those new to the field, as they embark on their journey in scientific writing. Additionally, understanding and embracing our roles in manuscript preparation and publication, whether as students or laboratory leaders (supervisors), is paramount. Chapter 3 will provide a detailed examination of these roles.

While numerous books on scientific writing have focused on techniques and language formalities, few, if any, have approached the writing process from the perspective of student-supervisor collaboration. In Chapter 4, we will delineate the ten essential steps towards achieving successful publication in collaboration with a supervisor, recognizing this collaborative dynamic as central to scientific writing.

Chapters 5 and 6 will offer comprehensive guidance on crafting research manuscripts and review papers, respectively. These manuscript types represent the cornerstone of scientific communication and merit special attention. These chapters will not only address the structural nuances of these manuscript formats but also provide practical advice on approaching their composition.

Effective scientific writing also entails a profound sense of ethical responsibility. As authors and researchers, it is imperative that we adhere to ethical standards from the outset of our research endeavors. Chapter 7 will delve into the intricacies of ethical considerations in publication, providing readers with the latest guidelines and insights into their roles as authors. However, writing alongside a supervisor may present its challenges. Nonetheless, maintaining awareness of available support resources can greatly facilitate the writing process. Chapter 8 will outline a comprehensive list of resources for assistance.

Chapter 2 The History Of Peer Review And Its Recent Process

The history

Understanding the origins of peer review is crucial for comprehending the entire process. The historical trajectory of manuscript peer review, depicted in Figure 2.1 (Spier, 2002), seems to have evolved gradually from the earliest works of Hippocrates and Aristotle over 2300 years ago. In that period, written documents did not undergo peer review;

nonetheless, the preservation of knowledge through the written word has withstood the test of time.

The history of peer review

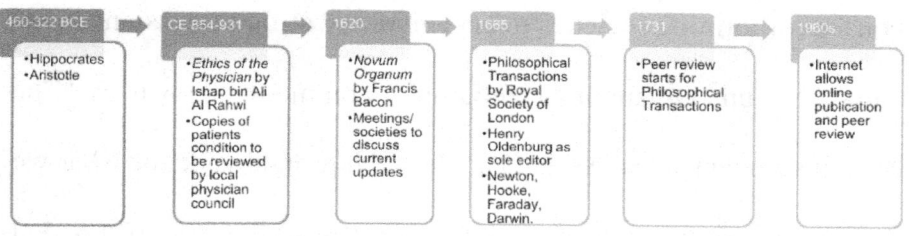

460-322 BCE	CE 854-931	1620	1665	1731	1960s
•Hippocrates •Aristotle	•*Ethics of the Physician* by Ishap bin Ali Al Rahwi •Copies of patients condition to be reviewed by local physician council	•*Novum Organum* by Francis Bacon •Meetings/ societies to discuss current updates	•Philosophical Transactions by Royal Society of London •Henry Oldenburg as sole editor •Newton, Hooke, Faraday, Darwin.	•Peer review starts for Philosophical Transactions	•Internet allows online publication and peer review

Figure 2.1 The history of manuscript peer review, as described by Spier (2002).

The earliest documented instance of peer review dates back to the period between CE 854-931, attributed to an individual from the Middle East. Ishap bin Ali-Al Rahwi from Syria, in his book "Ethics of the Physician," outlined the practice of transcribing and reviewing medical notes written by doctors about their patients by a local council of physicians. This approach allowed the council to evaluate the appropriateness of treatments and, in the unfortunate event of a patient's demise, these notes served as evidence for judgment.

Around 700 years later, in 1620, Francis Bacon introduced the concept of forming societies to engage in scientific discussions in his work "Novum Organum Scientiarum," commonly known as "The New Instrument of Science." This laid the groundwork for what we now know as conferences. Later, The Royal Society of London pioneered the establishment of a dedicated journal. In 1665, the world's first journal, "Philosophical Transactions," was inaugurated, and it continues to be in existence today. Initially, the review process for this journal was overseen solely by the editor, Henry Oldenburg, or his available colleagues. The actual peer review process for this journal commenced in 1731. During that time, as one would expect, most review processes were conducted through letters and physical mail. It was only after 200 years, with the advent of the internet, that quicker review processes with broader reviewer coverage became feasible. Notably, the journal attracted contributions from distinguished researchers such as Newton, Hooke, Faraday, and Darwin, underscoring its influential role within the scientific community.

During that era, most journals operated on a subscription basis, necessitating researchers and institutions to pay for access to specific journals of interest. In 2001, PLOS (Public Library of Science) launched the first fully Open Access journal, enabling authors to cover the dissemination costs of their articles to readers worldwide (https://www.plos.org/history). In recent years, a global initiative named "Plan S" has been introduced with the objective of ensuring that all research papers are accessible online through Open Access publications.

Recent process of peer review

The contemporary process of manuscript review commences with the submission of a completed document by an author or group of authors

(Figure 2.2). Following the selection of a suitable journal, the editor evaluates the manuscript's relevance and quality to ascertain its suitability for publication. Should the manuscript fall outside the journal's scope, be inadequately written, or contain significant scientific errors, it will face outright rejection. While this may seem stringent, facing rejection after an extensive review process can be even more disheartening. If the editor deems the manuscript worthy, they will assign at least two reviewers who are experts in the subject area under study. Though the corresponding author may suggest potential reviewers during submission, the editor may already possess a list of potential reviewers. Once the appointed reviewers agree to assess the paper, they are given a few weeks to complete the process.

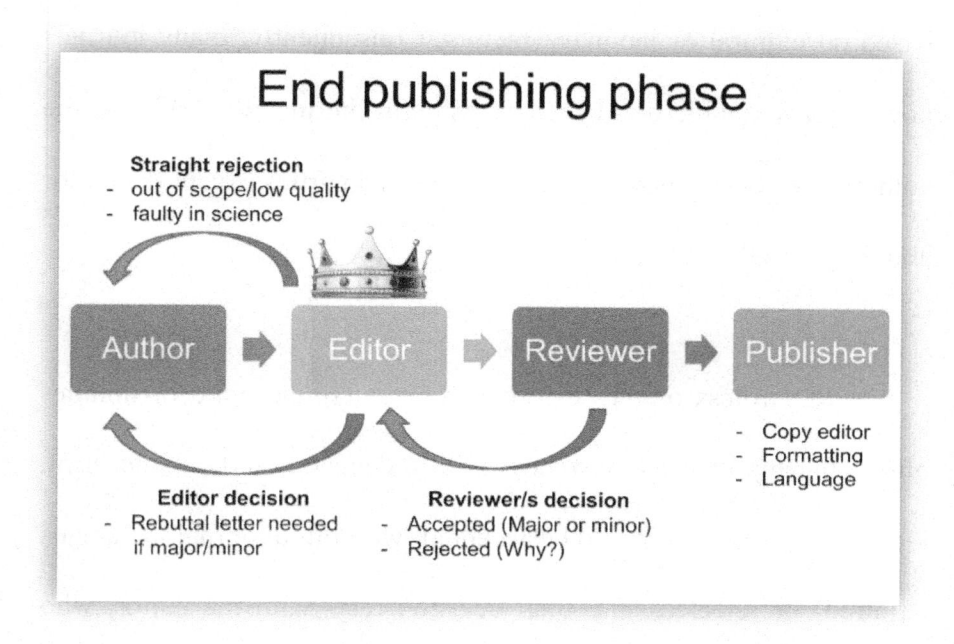

Figure 2.2 The end phase of publishing scientific manuscripts involves the editor, who plays a pivotal role (hence the crown depicted in the figure) in making decisions regarding submitted manuscripts.

Typically, there are two forms of the review process: single-blind and double-blind review. In single-blind review, the reviewers are aware of the authors' details, such as their names or affiliations, while the authors remain unaware of the reviewers' identities. However, this approach may introduce biases towards the authors based on cultural or language factors. Consequently, many journals now employ double-blind review, wherein the identities of both the authors and reviewers are concealed from all parties except the editor and the journal's staff.

Regardless of the reviewing format (single-blind or double-blind), the appointed reviewers provide a decision on the manuscript, indicating whether it should be accepted (with minor or major changes required) or rejected. The final decision rests with the editor, who takes into account the reviewers' feedback. If the reviewers believe the manuscript has potential for improvement, the authors are granted several weeks to revise the paper. Accompanying the revised manuscript, the authors are required to prepare a rebuttal letter outlining the changes that have been made. Upon reviewing these revisions, if the editor is satisfied, they may promptly make a decision to accept the paper. Alternatively, if further refinement is needed, another round of the review process ensues, repeating until the editor is satisfied. Once the manuscript is accepted, it undergoes typesetting and final adjustments in terms of formatting and language by the journal publisher's copyeditor. The authors are then given the opportunity to review the nearly polished manuscript and identify any errors, which are subsequently corrected before the final publication of the manuscript.

It is important to highlight that the reviewing process mentioned earlier relates specifically to the "end publishing phase". Equally significant is the initial stage of drafting and refining manuscripts between students and supervisors (depicted in Figure 2.3). This phase is particularly crucial in this book as it seeks to meet the requirements of students aiming for manuscript publication. The roles of each author, whether they are students, primary supervisors, or co-supervisors/authors, will be explored further in Chapter 3.

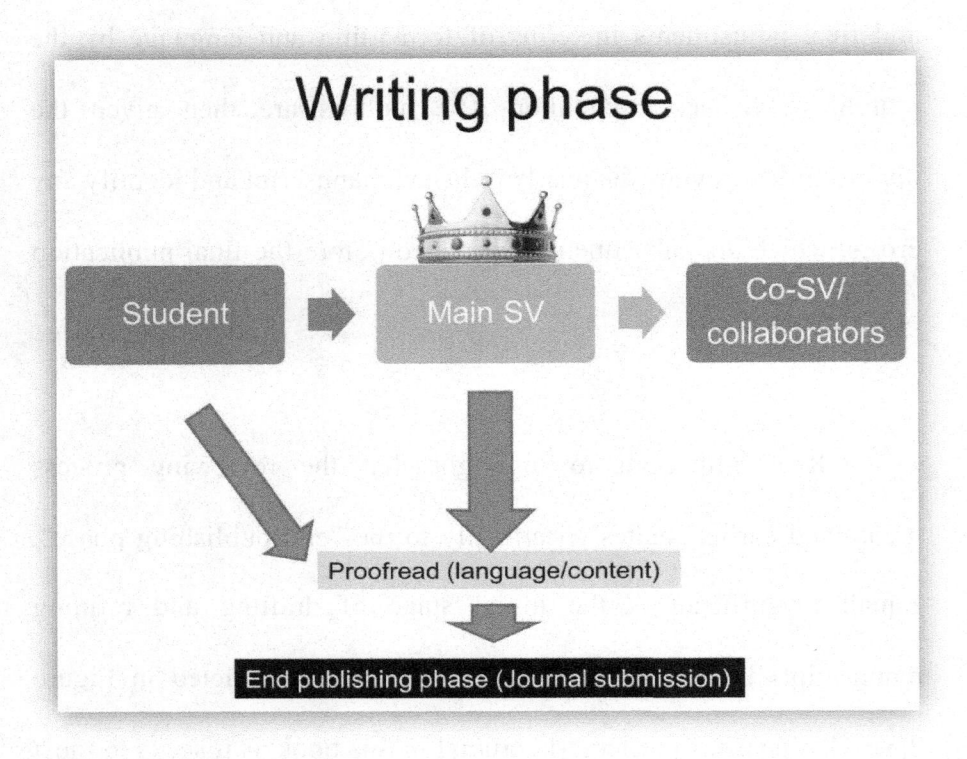

Figure 2.3 The writing phase of a scientific publication. The main supervisor (SV) plays a crucial role in determining the fate of the manuscript.

Chapter 3 Roles, Challenges And Expectations Of Students And Supervisors During Scientific Writing

Roles of students and supervisors

In the pursuit of success in manuscript writing, two fundamental rules emerge. The first rule dictates that "the limit is set by you (students)," while the second rule posits that "the subsequent limit is set by your supervisor(s)." These rules underscore the indispensable roles played by both students and supervisors in the process of effective manuscript writing. Although there may be instances where one party completes the paper without the involvement of the other, such a process tends to be protracted and may potentially necessitate extensive rewriting of the entire paper at a later stage.

Understanding the disparities between serving as a lecturer/supervisor at a higher institution and a school teacher (as outlined in Table 3.1) is crucial. This comprehension enables us to grasp the difficulties and challenges encountered by professionals in these respective domains. Teaching at the school level typically entails interaction with teenagers, while lecturers engage with young adults in universities and colleges. Consequently, the learning dynamics in schools and higher education institutions can vary significantly. In schools, assignments often come with grading and potential repercussions for incomplete work. Conversely, in university settings, particularly in postgraduate research studies, the emphasis leans towards self-governance and personal accountability. While school teachers may not concentrate on refining and publishing written work, lecturers play a role in aiding students in completing manuscripts for publication or theses.

Table 3.1 Similarities and differences between a school teacher and a lecturer/supervisor.

Aspects/ Criteria	School Teacher	Lecturer/ Supervisor
Student Types	Teenagers	Young adults
Place	School	University/colleges
Assignment	Will punish students if not completed	Punishing is beyond jurisdiction
Marks	Yes	Yes (for undergraduate and coursework) No (for postgraduate by research)

Lesson	Mostly spoon-feeding	Mostly autonomous
Writing	Will not perfect a writing	Will/should help to perfect a writing

Having discerned the disparities between the higher education system, comprising universities and colleges, and the schooling system, it becomes imperative to grasp the distinct roles and obligations assumed by postgraduate students and their supervisors throughout the manuscript writing process. These roles and obligations are encapsulated in Table 3.2.

Table 3.2 The distinct roles of postgraduate students and supervisors during the manuscript write-up process.

Postgraduate Students	**Supervisors**

• Finish up experimentation to complete a manuscript	• Discuss and decide experimental design with students
• Analyse and present data accurately and reasonably	• Check accuracy of presented data (and publishable)
• Come up with a first draft and perfecting it	• Check drafts critically within reasonable time
• Communicate and update supervisors regularly	• Communicate effectively with students, co-authors, proof-readers and editors

Postgraduate students are tasked with conducting and concluding the requisite experiments that contribute to a comprehensive manuscript. They are entrusted with overseeing the experimental process to ensure its seamless execution. Conversely, supervisors play a pivotal role in furnishing clear directives and guidance from the proposal writing phase onwards. Their expertise and guidance in experimental design are pivotal in shaping the overarching research trajectory.

Furthermore, it falls upon students to accurately analyse and present their experimental findings in a coherent and persuasive manner suitable for publication. However, supervisors bear the additional responsibility of meticulously scrutinising and validating the accuracy and suitability of the data for publication. Once the complete dataset is acquired, students are expected to draft the manuscript and refine it through subsequent iterations until it is primed for submission to a journal of interest. Throughout this process, supervisors should adhere to a reasonable timeframe for response, diligently reading and furnishing constructive feedback on the manuscript drafts. It is noteworthy that protracted delays in providing feedback can deflate students' motivation, impeding their progress and enthusiasm for manuscript completion.

In addition to their core duties, effective and consistent communication between students and supervisors is imperative. This transparent channel of communication facilitates the exchange of ideas, clarification of queries, and overall progress monitoring. Supervisors also bear the responsibility of orchestrating communication with co-authors, proof-readers, and editors, ensuring a seamless and successful publication journey.

Challenges during the publication process

While the roles of postgraduate students and supervisors in the publication journey are clearly defined, this endeavour is not devoid of challenges. Table 3.3 provides a comprehensive overview of the common problems encountered by both students and supervisors during manuscript writing. Though not exhaustive, it encompasses the major issues associated with the publication process.

Table 3.3 Writing issues from the perspectives of students and supervisors.

Student Point Of View	Supervisor Point Of View
Does not know where/what/how to start as well as no idea and motivation (writer's block)	Draft is not of the highest quality (in terms of content, depth and breadth)
Incomplete experimentation	Draft contains too many technical errors (typos, language issues)
Technical difficulties in word processing, citation manager and statistical tools	No urgency in finishing up experiments and writing
Language barrier and too harsh comments from supervisors	Too slow in finalising drafts
Supervisor is not an expert in subject area and late in returning drafts	Communication breakdown

For postgraduate students, one of the initial hurdles often lies in the lack of clarity on how and where to commence the manuscript writing process. This challenge will be extensively addressed in the forthcoming chapter (Chapter 4), which offers guidance on initiating the writing journey. Additionally, students may encounter writer's block, experiencing a dearth of motivation and struggling to generate ideas to complete the manuscript. Incomplete experiments and technical deficiencies, such as inadequate knowledge and proficiency in utilising word processing, citation management, and statistical tools, can also impede successful writing. Language barriers pose a significant problem, particularly in non-native English-speaking countries, as effectively conveying messages and ideas through writing becomes a bottleneck. Furthermore, students may face demotivation when subjected to overly harsh criticism from supervisors, encounter supervisors who lack expertise in the subject area and therefore provide inadequate critical feedback, or experience delays in receiving reviewed drafts due to supervisors' demanding schedules.

From the perspective of supervisors, challenges arise when dealing with manuscript drafts of low quality in terms of content depth and breadth. Technical errors, including typos and language deficiencies, may be prevalent and require extensive editing and revision. Another challenge faced by supervisors is students' lack of urgency in completing experiments, resulting in slow progress in manuscript write-up. However, perhaps one of the most detrimental challenges is a breakdown in communication between students and supervisors, which can result in a disastrous writing experience.

In the realm of manuscript writing, supervisors and students often grapple with a myriad of commitments and engagements that occupy their time. Table 3.4 offers a comprehensive insight into the various factors contributing to their hectic schedules. By discerning these perspectives, we can gain a deeper understanding of the obstacles encountered in manuscript completion.

Table 3.4 Common reasons for busy schedules among supervisors and students.

Students	Supervisor
Finishing up experiments, reading and writing	Teaching classes
Request from supervisor is endless (sometimes out of the project scope)	Several research projects to manage (different student supervision, grant reports)
Going to conferences and meetings	Attending/organizing conferences and meetings
Supervising other students	Being a reviewer for journals
Managing laboratory and work space	University requirements such as publicity and commercialization
Family	Family

From the student's standpoint, numerous responsibilities demand their attention. Engaging in experiments, extensive reading, and writing endeavours constitute time-consuming endeavours that students must prioritise. Moreover, attending conferences and meetings to enrich their knowledge and network is imperative for their academic development. However, students may encounter challenges when supervisors inundate them with incessant requests that extend beyond the confines of their project. Furthermore, unexpectedly assuming the role of supervising other students in the laboratory, alongside managing their own workspace and tasks, can prove overwhelming. Striking a balance amidst these responsibilities poses a considerable challenge.

Conversely, supervisors encounter a distinct set of hurdles. Teaching obligations often consume a substantial portion of their time, diverting their focus from research endeavours. Juggling multiple projects with varying student supervision requirements adds further intricacy to their schedules. Additionally, supervisors may find themselves immersed in coordinating and attending conferences and meetings, as well as serving as reviewers for academic journals. Moreover, universities may impose additional mandates on supervisors, such as bolstering publicity efforts and spearheading commercialisation initiatives to generate revenue. These supplementary responsibilities detract from their primary research endeavours.

Despite these divergent challenges, both supervisors and students share a common facet—family. They hold their loved ones in high regard and strive to strike a harmonious balance between professional commitments and familial responsibilities. Achieving this equilibrium becomes a crucial consideration in their bustling lives.

Managing expectation

In the realm of scientific writing, students and supervisors often hold divergent expectations, leading to potential discord and dissatisfaction. Students may envisage their supervisors providing comprehensive guidance, including strategies to target prestigious journals such as Nature, and delineating every aspect of the writing process. Conversely, supervisors may anticipate students to exhibit autonomy and produce a high-calibre paper independently.

Such contrasting expectations can breed tension and impede fruitful collaboration. Hence, it is imperative to establish a shared understanding of the desired attributes and roles of exemplary students and supervisors in scientific writing. This delineation will serve as a roadmap for both parties, nurturing a more constructive and harmonious working dynamic (Table 3.5).

Table 3.5 Characteristics of ideal students and supervisors from both perspectives.

Ideal Students (From Supervisor's Perspectives)	Ideal Supervisor (From Student's Perspectives)

Being independent, discuss experimental design and execute it appropriately	Responsible, dedicated, responsive and ethical
Able to present and analyse data using appropriate statistics	Academically, technically and financially sound/strong
Adequate knowledge in the project to allow effective communication (writing and orally)	Vast networking
Critical in discussion (written and orally)	Giving insightful comments
Proficient language use	Motivator and counsellor, emotionally stable
Proficient user of MS word, excel, statistical and referencing tools	Team player
Polite and well mannered	Treat students justly
Hardworking genius	Supportive

There are various attributes deemed ideal for both students and supervisors, depending on their respective roles and perspectives. For instance, an exemplary student should demonstrate traits such as independence, critical thinking skills, and the ability to discuss and implement experimental designs effectively. Proficiency in data presentation and analysis, particularly in statistical contexts, is also essential. Moreover, students should possess adequate knowledge and skills relevant to their projects, enabling them to communicate proficiently through both written scientific discourse and oral presentations. Therefore, the capacity for engaging in critical discussions and utilising proficient language skills, both in their native tongue and in English, is paramount. Additionally, ideal students are adept users of various tools such as MS Word, Excel, image editing software, and statistical and referencing tools. Moreover, academic excellence coupled with politeness and good manners is appreciated. In essence, supervisors highly value diligent and talented individuals in their laboratories.

Conversely, exemplary supervisors are characterized by their responsibility, dedication, responsiveness, and ethical conduct. They must possess robust academic and technical acumen, as well as sound financial stability to support students throughout their research endeavours. Additionally, supervisors should have extensive networks to address any issues or challenges faced by their students by connecting them with appropriate resources. Ideal supervisors consistently provide insightful feedback, particularly regarding their students' progress and writing, while also serving as motivators and mentors. These supervisors, driven by a strong sense of altruism, regard their students as team members, fostering mutual growth. Lastly, exceptional supervisors engage in occasional outings with their students to foster social connections.

An article published in Science suggests that outstanding supervisors exhibit specific characteristics, including strong support for student progress, shared work ethics, and prestige (source:

https://www.sciencemag.org/careers/2019/04/what-matters-phd-adviser-here-s-what-research-says?utm_campaign=ScienceNow&utm_source=JHubbard&utm_medium=Facebook). Supervisors who provide adequate support, without excessively micromanaging their students, cultivate independence among researchers within their labs. Moreover, supervisors whose work habits and styles align with those of their students can significantly contribute to their research endeavours. Finally, supervisors with expertise in a specific research area are likely to assist their graduated students in securing research or academic positions elsewhere. However, when comparing these characteristics, it is evident that supportive behaviour is the most critical aspect valued by research graduates.

It is noteworthy that there is currently a dearth of academic programmes dedicated specifically to coaching individuals on how to excel as supervisors or students. Regarding students, their proficiency in scientific inquiry and research is often intertwined with their intrinsic motivation and natural inclinations. Those who exhibit strong perseverance are more inclined to persist and potentially advance into principal investigators and scientists in the future. As for supervisors, many of them rely on their own experiences as former students and strive to replicate the teaching methodologies of their own mentors. However, concerning the domain of writing, there exist various approaches through which supervisors and students can undergo training to enhance their skills, thus complementing each other's abilities. These approaches will be expounded upon in the forthcoming chapter entitled "The 10 Steps of Successful Writing with Your Supervisors."

Chapter 4 The 10 Steps Of Successful Writing With Your Supervisors

The art of writing, akin to numerous other skills, is both learnable and teachable. While the majority of literature in this domain tends to concentrate on crafting scientific manuscripts, there is a noticeable dearth of resources focusing on the intricacies of collaborative writing with supervisors. This aspect is arguably one of the most pivotal components in achieving successful writing outcomes. Consequently, this section delineates the 10 Steps of Successful Writing with Your Supervisors presented in Figure 4.1.

STEPS

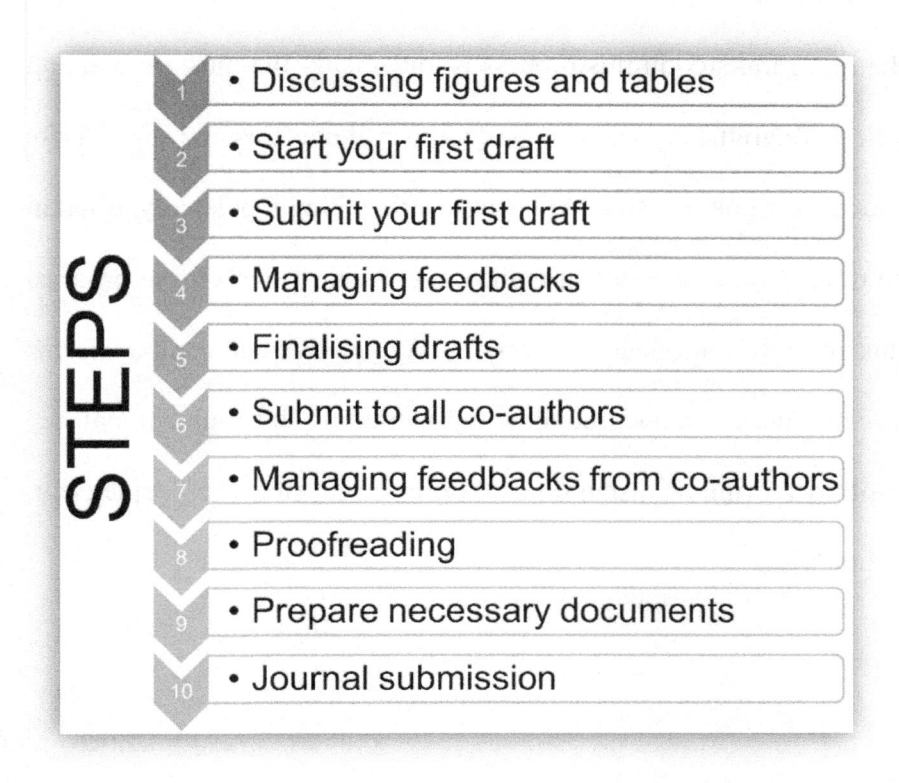

1. Discussing figures and tables
2. Start your first draft
3. Submit your first draft
4. Managing feedbacks
5. Finalising drafts
6. Submit to all co-authors
7. Managing feedbacks from co-authors
8. Proofreading
9. Prepare necessary documents
10. Journal submission

Figure 4.1 The 10 steps for successful publication with your supervisors.

Step 1

The inaugural step in this process is undeniably the most pivotal and critical. Regrettably, a substantial number of students and supervisors tend to overlook this step, with some undertaking it belatedly, often in the middle or, worse, towards the conclusion of the writing process. This not only complicates matters for both parties but also transforms the experience into one fraught with frustration. This foundational step involves the initial discussion of figures and tables, as depicted in Figure 4.2.

Step 1: Discussing figures and tables

- Take home message
- Order of figures and tables
- Example published manuscript
- Accuracy and publishable
- Experimental design
- Statistics

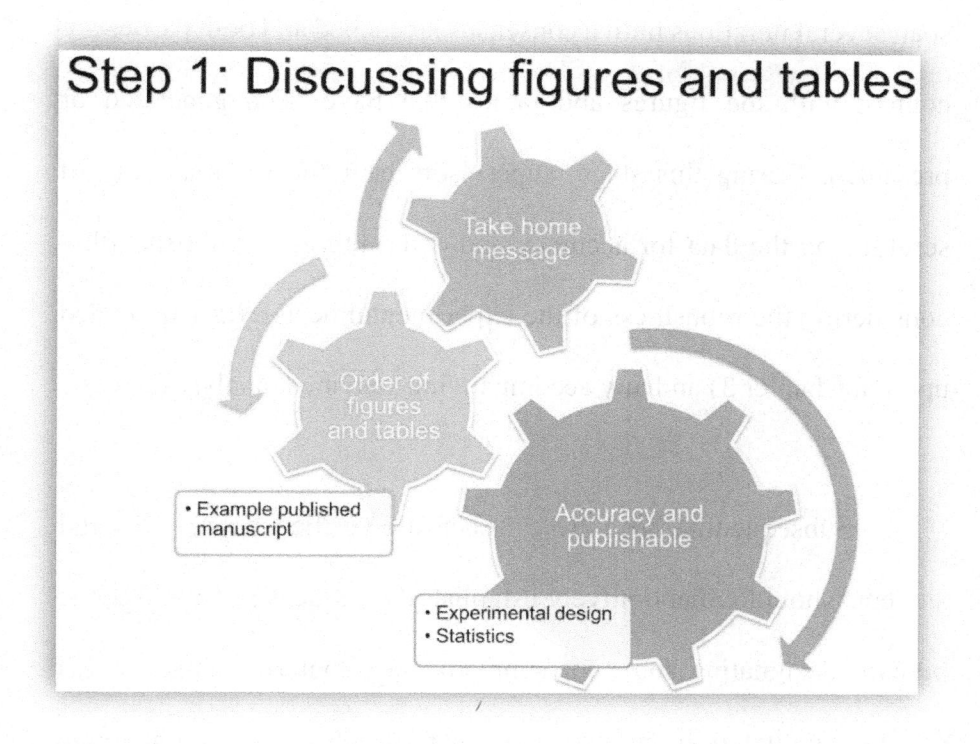

Figure 4.2 The primary stride towards achieving a successful publication involves initiating a discussion with the supervisor regarding the specifics of figures and tables prior to embarking on the actual writing process.

Primarily, students and their supervisors must convene to deliberate on the potential presentation of data. This discussion may span several iterations until a consensus is reached and both parties are content with the figures and tables that have been generated or presented. During this stage, supervisors bear the responsibility of scrutinizing the data for accuracy and determining its publishability, considering the robustness of the experimental design (as expounded upon in Chapter 3) and any accompanying statistical analyses.

Subsequently, once these aspects are verified, supervisors and students should collaboratively establish the sequence of the figures, perhaps designating some for supplementary material. This process can be facilitated if an exemplar manuscript from a comparable experiment is available (sourced from a target journal). In instances where no such example exists, joint decisions should be made, with paramount consideration given to aligning the included figures and tables with the manuscript's overarching message. It is crucial to note that there might be occasions when the primary supervisor lacks expertise in the specific subject matter of the paper. In such scenarios, it is imperative to seek assistance from individuals with relevant experience, as remaking figures, tables, and written content at the later stages could prove detrimental to both the paper and the motivation of the student.

Step 2

Upon the comprehensive representation of data through figures and tables, the subsequent step involves the commencement of the initial draft by the students. It is not uncommon for students to encounter moments of feeling "out of ideas" or experiencing a "mental block." However, the assurance lies in the completion of the preliminary step to mutual satisfaction, which substantially diminishes the likelihood of encountering such challenges. Nevertheless, should the need arise, writers can refer to numerous writing books available in the market, including the valuable insights shared by my esteemed lecturer and teacher, Margaret Cargill, from whom I had the privilege to learn during my PhD studies. Cargill's book, titled "Writing Scientific Research Articles: Strategy and Steps," serves as a comprehensive guide outlining fundamental principles for formulating and completing scientific writing. Additional strategies and tips for drafting research articles and review papers are revealed upon in Chapters 5 and 6, respectively.

In my personal approach (as depicted in Figure 4.3), the key to initiating and sustaining the writing process lies in one crucial factor—motivation. To effectively tackle this challenge, I advocate for starting with the easier sections before progressing to the more complex ones. Drawing an analogy to exam-taking, where challenging questions are often skipped and revisited later, I begin by composing a complete Methods section. This approach is facilitated by the prior discussion with our supervisor regarding the order of the figures, ensuring a seamless flow. Typically, content for this section is derived from laboratory notes or paraphrased from relevant manuscripts, rendering the process relatively straightforward and serving as a motivational catalyst. While subsequent sections are of lesser significance, revisiting the Methods section during moments of demotivation serves as a powerful reminder of the substantial progress made in the paper. Finally, the elusive Discussion section beckons. Writing a compelling Discussion hinges on a profound understanding of the results. The depth of comprehension is nurtured through critical engagement with related manuscripts. It is imperative to cultivate a sense of originality and be unafraid to express unique ideas. Despite apprehensions about potential ridicule from supervisors, it is crucial to recognize that groundbreaking innovations often arise from initially dismissed ideas. As long as the discussion adheres to scientific correctness and logic, the exploration of novel perspectives is not only acceptable but also commendable.

Step 2: Start your first draft

Start with the easiest section
Materials & Methods

End with the hardest section
Discussion

Microsoft Office skills
Effective writing, data analysis

Figure 4.3 The second step in the journey towards successful writing entails commencing the first draft with a well-thought-out plan and the requisite skills.

Another determinant of successful writing lies in the proficiency of the writer's skills. The potency and utility of advanced Microsoft Office skills (or other similar tools), often underestimated, wield considerable influence in enhancing the writing process. Software applications like Word, Excel, and PowerPoint can prove to be invaluable tools for writers. From a student's perspective, mastery of these applications should extend beyond the rudimentary level to encompass intermediate and advanced levels. This heightened proficiency not only contributes to improved writing but also enhances capabilities in data analysis. Consequently, it becomes a driving force for elevating the quality of writing and overall productivity.

Step 3

Moving on to the next step, the completed draft is now ready for submission to our supervisor or supervisors. However, a common challenge faced by many students is the delayed response from their supervisors. To preemptively address this issue, it is advisable to inquire about the availability of your supervisor at least one week before the scheduled submission (Figure 4.4). This proactive approach ensures that they can allocate sufficient time to review the draft promptly.

Step 3: Submit your first draft

- Ask availability
- Hardcopy preference
- Remind after 7-10 days

Figure 4.4 Step 3 entails the submission of your initial draft to the principal supervisor.

Additionally, it is crucial to ascertain your supervisor's preference for reviewing drafts—whether they prefer a hard copy or are comfortable with electronic versions for reading and commenting.

Following the submission, a gentle reminder after around 7 to 10 days may be warranted. This serves as a nudge, particularly if the write-up is not at the forefront of their to-do list and may have slipped from their immediate attention. Expressing enthusiasm about progressing with the paper can be instrumental in eliciting a swift response from supervisors, as your dedication is likely to resonate with them and prompt a reciprocal commitment to your paper's needs.

Step 4

The subsequent phase in the writing process is arguably one of the most challenging situations we encounter—managing feedback (refer to Figure 4.5). In the initial draft, it is expected that the supervisor's input, represented by copious annotations and comments, will surpass our own contributions. This influx of red marks and remarks may initially be demotivating. The key strategy is to read through all the comments and then allow a day's break before addressing them. The first reading often induces a challenging emotional response, making it difficult to focus on substantial improvements. A day of respite enables constructive planning to take place subconsciously. Upon returning the next day, the comments may seem more manageable, facilitating a more effective response.

Step 4: Managing feedbacks

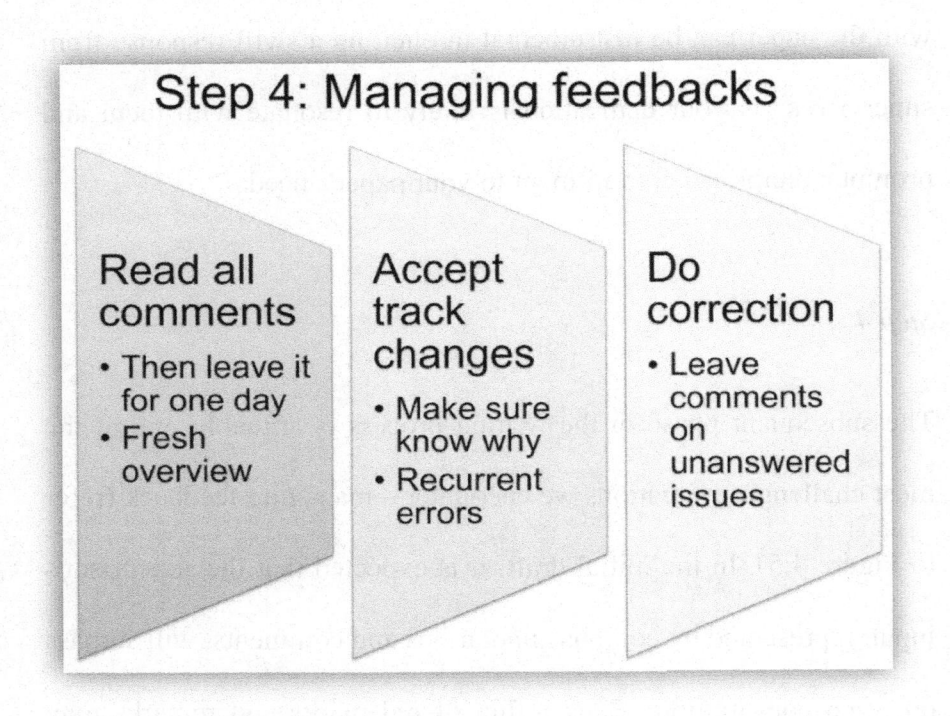

Read all comments
- Then leave it for one day
- Fresh overview

Accept track changes
- Make sure know why
- Recurrent errors

Do correction
- Leave comments on unanswered issues

Figure 4.5 Step 4 involves the crucial process of managing feedback from your supervisor.

While incorporating changes, it is essential to understand the reasons behind each comment. Some may be indicative of recurring language errors, and comprehending these nuances is vital for preventing repetition. Commence the process by addressing and modifying the comments, ensuring that you have not only accepted the tracked changes but also understood the underlying issues. Before removing comments, verify that each one has been adequately addressed. If a comment remains unaddressed, it is prudent to leave a response indicating the specific problem or challenge. This approach ensures that your supervisor is aware of your difficulties, fostering a collaborative atmosphere where assistance can be provided as needed.

Step 5

Moving on to Step 5, the finalization of the paper involves a cyclical process, reiterating Steps 3 and 4 (refer to Figure 4.6). This iterative approach is crucial and continues until both the writer and the supervisor are content with the quality of the manuscript.

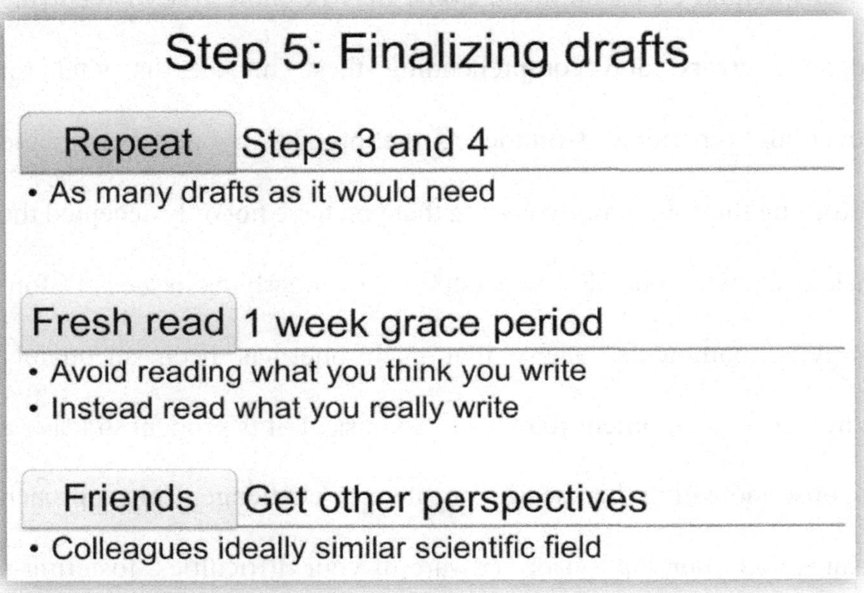

Step 5: Finalizing drafts

Repeat | Steps 3 and 4
- As many drafts as it would need

Fresh read | 1 week grace period
- Avoid reading what you think you write
- Instead read what you really write

Friends | Get other perspectives
- Colleagues ideally similar scientific field

Figure 4.6 In Step 5, the finalization of the draft is achieved by revisiting and repeating the processes outlined in the earlier Steps 3 and 4.

The number of drafts required to complete a manuscript can vary based on several factors, including the paper's intended impact (aiming for high impact factor journals may necessitate more extensive writing), the quantity of presented data (more data often entails more challenging discussions and conceptualization), the writer's skills (language proficiency can be a significant task for some), and the reviewing skills and time commitments of the supervisor. While practice and experience can expedite this process, patience remains paramount in achieving a well-crafted piece.

Upon reaching the final draft, it is advisable to withhold the paper for approximately one week before revisiting it. This deliberate pause allows for a fresh reading experience, as being deeply immersed in the manuscript may lead to reading what we think is written, rather than what is actually on the page. Another effective strategy for enhancing writing quality involves having someone other than yourself or your supervisor review the paper. Colleagues, especially those in the laboratory, can offer valuable perspectives. A few treats or gestures of appreciation might motivate them to provide constructive feedback, contributing to refining the draft before progressing to the next stage.

Step 6

Ensuring that all co-authors thoroughly read your paper is crucial to avoid potential issues later on. Neglecting this step can lead to mistakes in names and disagreements over scientific arguments. Despite the pride associated with having their names on the paper, all authors must recognize that ethical considerations and potential misconduct are collective responsibilities borne by the entire list of authors. A detailed exploration of these ethical aspects will be provided in the forthcoming chapter.

To secure a timely response from co-authors, proactive measures should be taken, as illustrated in Figure 4.7. Notifying them a couple of weeks before sending the final draft allows them to adjust their schedules accordingly. Another effective strategy is understanding the priority list of authors. Those who specialize in the field of the paper should be given priority, as they can provide early comments on technical aspects. Subsequently, the paper can be passed on to authors who are more focused on language considerations. This sequencing minimizes the need for multiple rounds of rewriting and reediting. It is also important to inquire about their preference for receiving the manuscript, whether in softcopy or hardcopy, and establish a dedicated deadline for their review.

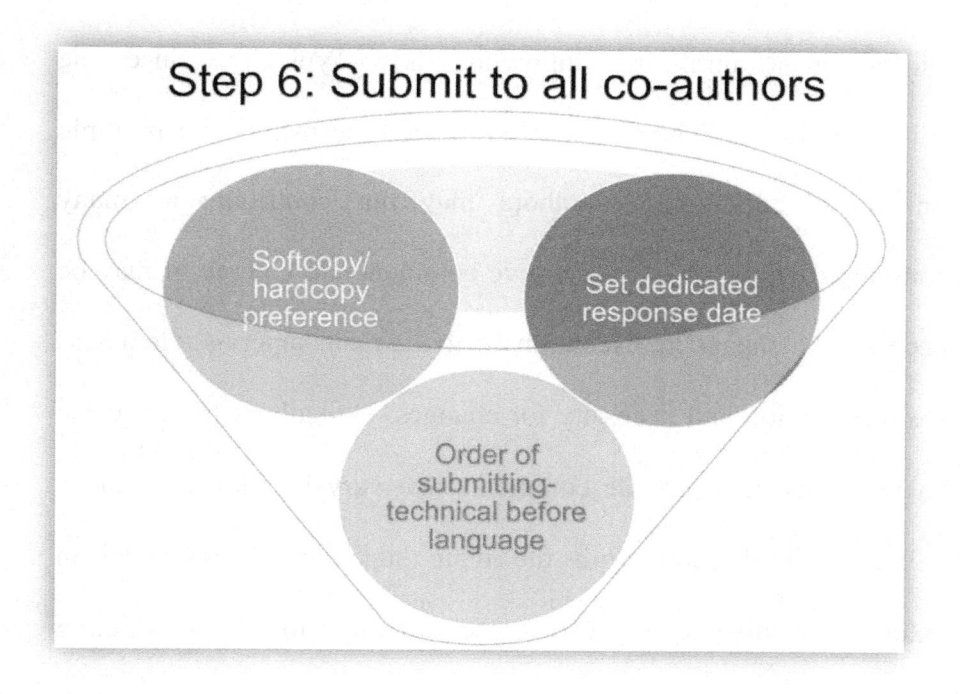

Figure 4.7 In Step 6, the manuscript is submitted to all co-authors for their thorough review and input.

Step 7

This step, depicted in Figure 4.8, closely mirrors Step 4 from earlier in the process. As customary, commence by thoroughly reading all the comments. If the feedback is extensive, it may be prudent to defer addressing it until the following day. Typically, since the corresponding author has likely scrutinized the manuscript multiple times, the additional co-authors may not contribute as many comments. However, if substantive comments do emerge, it may be necessary to engage in discussions with the main supervisor to assess the justification and necessity for changes. Co-authors from diverse backgrounds may provide comments that vary in relevance, and a collaborative decision with the main supervisor is essential in determining their merit. Pay close attention to any conflicting responses, and these should be verified and resolved in consultation with the main supervisor. Subsequently, accept the tracked changes and modify the manuscript as deemed appropriate. At this juncture, the manuscript is approximately 80% ready. If there is uncertainty about the language, consider sending it for proofreading, a step that will be detailed in the subsequent stage.

Step 7: Managing feedback from co-authors
- Read all comments first- then leave it for one day
- Consolidate conflicting responses- ask main supervisor
- Modify accordingly

Figure 4.8 Step 7 underscores the importance of managing feedback from co-authors.

Step 8

Proofreading, though optional, can be carried out interchangeably or concurrently with Step 9, which involves preparing necessary documents for journal submission, as will be detailed shortly. For those in the early stages of their research careers or new to scientific writing, it is advisable to consider checking for plagiarism (refer to Figure 4.9). Unintentional instances of plagiarism may occur during the writing process and can be detected using online tools such as Turnitin. However, access to such software often requires a subscription through the institute. Librarians can provide guidance on plagiarism checks, so it is recommended to consult them. Reputable journals typically conduct similar checks, and manuscripts showing high similarity to online content or other publications may be returned for rephrasing or outright rejection. The acceptable percentage of similarity varies, generally ranging from less than 10%, which is considered a decent level, to potentially less than 30%, depending on the journal.

Step 8: Proofreading

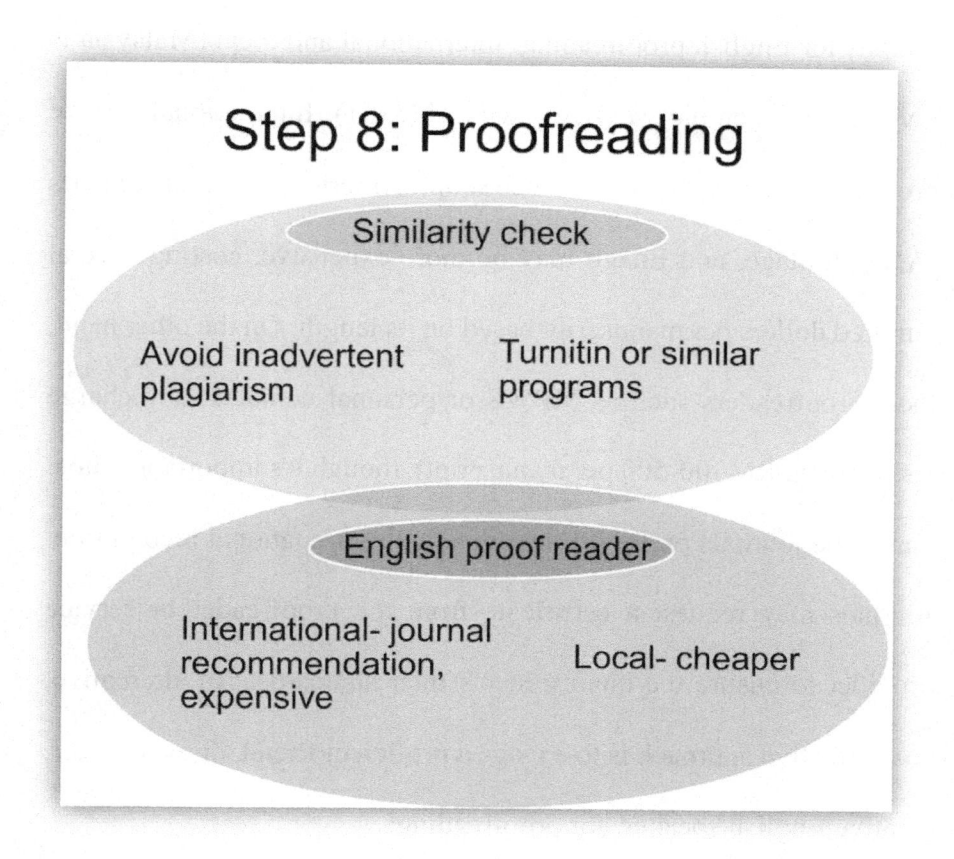

- Similarity check
  - Avoid inadvertent plagiarism
  - Turnitin or similar programs
- English proof reader
  - International- journal recommendation, expensive
  - Local- cheaper

Figure 4.9 In Step 8, proofreading takes center stage, addressing either similarity checks or language refinement.

Language checking is a critical aspect that editors often assess before sending a manuscript for review. Hence, it is prudent to undertake this process early to save valuable time. There are two options for English proofreading: international and local (Malaysia is given as an example) services (see Table 4.1). International service providers such as Elsevier WebShop, American Journal Experts (AJE), Editage, and Enago may be more expensive, costing several hundred dollars per manuscript based on its length. On the other hand, local proofreaders such as MPWS or personal contacts may charge less (around RM300-500 per manuscript), though it's important to note that some journals prefer proofreaders with international recognition. Journals may request a certificate from the proofreader or service provider to ensure the quality meets their standards. An alternative, cost-effective approach is to engage a proficient friend, or even better, a native English speaker, for proofreading.

Table 4.1 An approximate pricing overview for various English editing services from international and national (Malaysia is given as an example) companies as of April-May 2019. Please note that these prices may have changed, and it's advisable to check the respective websites for the most current information and service details.

Services	Price	Website
\multicolumn{3}{c}{National (Malaysia)}		
Proofreading by a UK PhD	RM25 (normal 12 days) & 30 per page (urgent 8 days) per page	https://www.facebook.com/proofreadingbyPhD/
MPWS	RM6.50 (normal 7 days) & RM14 (express 3 days) per page	http://www.proofandread.com/services.php
\multicolumn{3}{c}{International}		
Elsevier WebShop	USD285 (normal 7 days) & USD399 (express 3 days) per 6000 words	https://webshop.elsevier.com/languageservices/
American Journal Experts (AJE)	USD298 (normal 5 days) & USD473 (express 2 days) per 6000 words	https://www.aje.com/services/editing/

Editage	USD306 (normal 5 days) & USD396 (express 3 days) per 6000 words	https://www.editage.com/editing-services/manuscript-editing.html
Enago	USD120 (express 4 days) per 6000 words (only for native)	https://www.enago.com/proofreading.htm

Alternatively, if you are concerned about your English proficiency but seek a free and quick checking solution, consider using software tools. One such tool is Grammarly (https://www.grammarly.com/), which offers both an online submission tool and a desktop application to detect and provide advice on simple grammatical errors. Utilizing such tools as your initial step in refining your manuscript's language can offer significant benefits. Rectifying basic and avoidable mistakes is crucial, as such errors can be vexing for readers, particularly when your audience includes extremely busy supervisors.

Step 9

Step 9 involves the preparation of necessary documents (refer to Figure 4.10). While this may seem straightforward, it can be a time-consuming task, spanning a day or even several days. The first crucial step is to locate and thoroughly read the 'Instructions to Authors' provided on the journal's website. This is paramount, as most journals have specific quality and format requirements for submitted papers.

Step 9: Prepare necessary documents
- Interchangeably with Step 8
- Read "Instruction to Author"
- Formatting- references, sections
- Figure/table formatting
- Cover letter
- Others- highlights, abstract figure (if necessary)

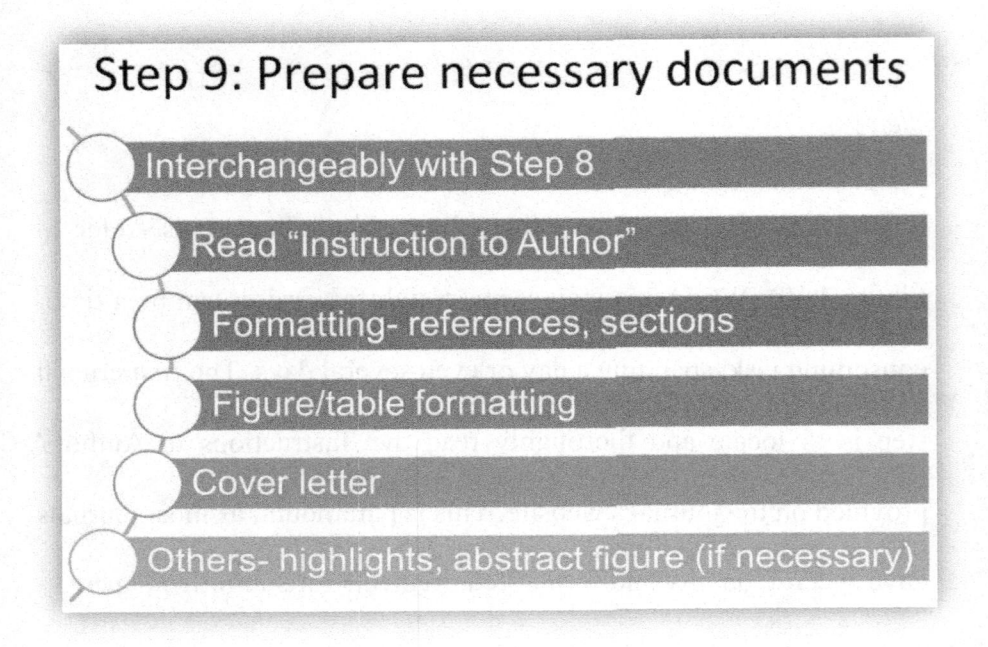

Figure 4.10 In Step 9, the focus is on the meticulous preparation of documents in accordance with the specific requirements of the chosen journal.

Common formatting issues include the reference style and the order of sections. Some journals may prefer the Methods section at the end, necessitating potential rewrites to seamlessly integrate it into the overall flow of the paper. Ensuring the figures and tables have the best resolution possible is also essential. A helpful strategy for formatting is to follow the style of a recent publication from the target journal. This provides a tangible example of the final form and facilitates the polishing of the manuscript.

Additionally, it's crucial to include a cover letter. This short letter to the editor articulates why the paper should be considered for publication in the journal. It should generate interest and entice the editor to review and potentially publish the paper. Some journals may require additional documents, such as highlights and abstract figures, so it is essential to carefully review their specific requirements.

Step 10

In Step 10, the culmination of the process involves submitting the manuscript to the chosen journal (refer to Figure 4.11). Submission procedures can vary, with many journals employing online submission systems, while some older journals may still prefer email submissions. Each submission system has its unique requirements. Some may ask for suggestions regarding potential reviewers or allow the author to express preferences against certain reviewers. However, the final decision on reviewers is typically made by the editor.

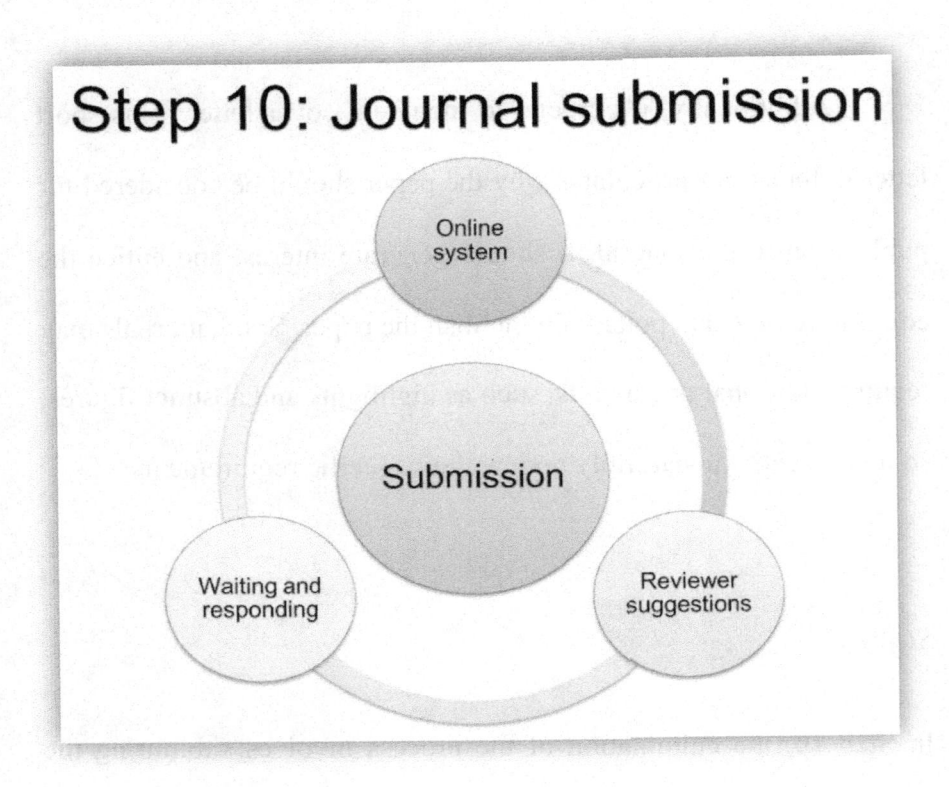

Step 10: Journal submission

- Online system
- Submission
- Waiting and responding
- Reviewer suggestions

Figure 4.11 The final step in achieving a successful publication with your supervisor is, indeed, the submission of the manuscript to the journal of interest.

Following submission, the subsequent phase involves a waiting game and responding to any queries or requests from reviewers or editors. This aspect has been discussed in detail in Chapter 2, and readers are encouraged to refer to that section for comprehensive insights into managing the peer review process.

Selecting the most appropriate journal for manuscript submission is a critical aspect of the process. Here are several strategies for making this decision:

1. Natural Alignment

Choose a journal that aligns naturally with the content of your manuscript. Often, during the writing process, you may find yourself citing certain journals more frequently. This could indicate a natural fit for your work.

2. Field-Based Selection

Consider the field or discipline of your research. Compile a list of reputable journals in your research area. Review recent publications in these journals to gauge the depth and detail of results presented.

3. Dedicated Websites:

Utilize dedicated websites that assist in journal selection based on your manuscript's title, abstract, and area of study. Examples include:

- Elsevier Journal Finder

(https://journalfinder.elsevier.com/)

- Springer Journal Suggestor

(https://journalsuggester.springer.com/)

- Wiley Journal Finder

(https://journalfinder.wiley.com/search?type=match)

These websites often provide a list of journals that are likely to consider and potentially accept your paper based on the information you input. Regardless of the method chosen, it's crucial to carefully review the scope, focus, and recent publications of the selected journals to ensure they are the best fit for your research.

Chapter 5 Strategy To Write A Research Manuscript

In the preceding chapter (Chapter 4), we acquired insights into the optimal practices for successfully navigating the publication of research articles in collaboration with a supervisor. Proficiency in reading, writing, and reviewing our own manuscript is paramount in facilitating the completion of initial drafts. However, for early career researchers and students, the challenge often lies in the decision-making process regarding potential manuscripts for publication. It is imperative to recognize that there exists a diverse array of paper types beyond research articles that hold the potential for publication. This chapter is dedicated to a comprehensive exploration of these various manuscript types.

Moreover, this chapter will meticulously examine the fundamental components intrinsic to research articles, namely the title, abstract, introduction, methods, discussion, and conclusion. Each of these components will undergo dissection, accompanied by the presentation of effective strategies to compose them. By understanding the nuances of each section and implementing strategic writing approaches, researchers can enhance the quality and impact of their manuscripts.

Manuscript types

It is crucial to recognize that various types of manuscripts exist, each serving distinct purposes (refer to Table 5.1). The primary category encompasses Research, Original, and Primary manuscripts. Following this, we have Review, Mini Review, Systematic Review, and Scoping Review papers constituting the second type of manuscripts. The third category involves Letters, Communications, and Brief Research Reports. The fourth type encompasses Opinion pieces, Commentaries, and Perspectives. Lastly, the fifth type includes Data and Methods articles. The choice among these manuscript types is significantly influenced by the preferences of the target journal.

Table 5.1 The various manuscript types, their attributes, and example journals (non-exhaustive) featuring them are detailed here. Predominantly situated in multidisciplinary domains, these journals ensure extensive applicability to both students and supervisors. It is pertinent to note that the specified word limits serve as approximations, given the potential divergence in guidelines among individual journals. PLoS, Public Library of Science; PNAS,

Proceedings of the National Academy of Sciences of the United States of America.

Type	Manuscript types	Attributes	Example journals
1	Research/ Original/ Primary manuscript	• Reporting original experimental data • Word limit: 4500-12,000 *Discussed in this Chapter 5	Nature, Science, Scientific Reports, PLoS, PNAS, PeerJ, Frontiers
2	Review/ Mini review/ Systematic review/ Scoping review	• Assessing literature exhaustively for comprehensive updates	Annual Reviews, Frontiers, Journal of Advanced Research, PeerJ

		• Word limit: 3000-10,000 *Discussed in Chapter 6	
3	Letters/ Communications/ Brief Research Reports	• Shorter or more compact version of Type 1 manuscripts • Word limit: 500-4000	Nature, PNAS
4	Opinion/ Commentaries/ Perspectives	• Short discussion about current findings and reports • Word limit: 1000-2000	Frontiers, Science, PNAS
5	Data/ Methods	• Reporting data or methods without	Data in Brief, F1000Research,

	elaborative discussion • Word limit: 3000- unlimited	Scientific data, GigaScience, MethodsX

While the Research manuscript (Type 1) is the most prevalent, detailing the outcomes of experiments and reporting research findings, it is noteworthy that certain journals provide alternatives (Table 5.1). This chapter will extensively elucidate the structure and sections of the Type 1 article, which typically incorporates a substantial number of figures and tables to comprehensively present data.

Within the realm of scholarly manuscripts, we encounter a distinct genre/type denoted as Type 2 manuscripts, specifically review articles. This category encompasses various manifestations, including mini reviews, systematic reviews, and scoping reviews. The prescribed word count for such articles spans between 3000 and 10,000 words, contingent upon the preferences of the targeted journal.

Noteworthy multidisciplinary journals that feature review articles include Annual Reviews (submission exclusively by invitation), Frontiers, Journal of Advanced Research, and PeerJ. Given the pivotal role of this manuscript variant as a primary form of scientific dissemination, an exhaustive examination will be undertaken in Chapter 6.

Conversely, the Type 3 article assumes the form of Letters, Communications, or Brief Research Reports. Distinguished by its succinct nature, it functions as a condensed iteration of the Type 1 article, eschewing the discrete sections found in the latter, such as introduction, methodology, and discussion (although a continuous flow exists between these segments, marked by discernible nuances). Esteemed journals of the highest echelon, including Nature and PNAS (Proceedings of the National Academy of Sciences of the United States of America), commonly publish manuscripts of this type due to constraints in available publication space. The prescribed word limit for Type 3 manuscripts ranges from 500 to 4000 words.

The fourth classification (Type 4) of manuscript pertains to Opinion, Commentaries, and Perspectives. This category predominantly involves the synthesis and discussion of contemporary findings or reports, particularly those relevant to specific topics of interest within broad communities. While this article type serves to apprise readers of recent developments or breakthroughs in the research domain, it may not attain the comprehensive scope of a full-fledged review article (Type 2). Its length is confined to approximately 1000-2000 words, and it finds publication in journals such as Frontiers, Science, and PNAS.

The ultimate and, perhaps, the most recent genre of manuscript (Type 5) revolves around Data or Method papers. Journals like Data in Brief, F1000Research, Scientific Data, GigaScience, and MethodsX predominantly provide authors with an alternative avenue to disseminate data typically incorporated in supplementary materials. This approach enhances data visibility, facilitating broader dissemination and encouraging experimental replication. One of the salient features of this manuscript type is its focus on reporting data or methods, presented without extensive discussion. Although the word limit can extend from 3000 words onwards, these manuscripts generally tend to be concise.

Understanding journal impact factor and quartile

Before delving into the technical intricacies of manuscript composition, it is imperative to grasp the mechanisms by which journals are indexed and evaluated for quality and popularity. A case in point is the impact factor of a journal, signifying the average annual citation count for cumulative manuscripts published by said journal. This metric is commonly employed by the indexing entity Web of Science to gauge the influence of a particular journal (refer to Figure 5.1). The impact factor is determined by dividing the total number of citations in the preceding two years by the number of articles published during that same period. To illustrate, an impact factor of 4 in 2019 indicates that, on average, the journal received four citations per manuscript over the years 2017 and 2018.

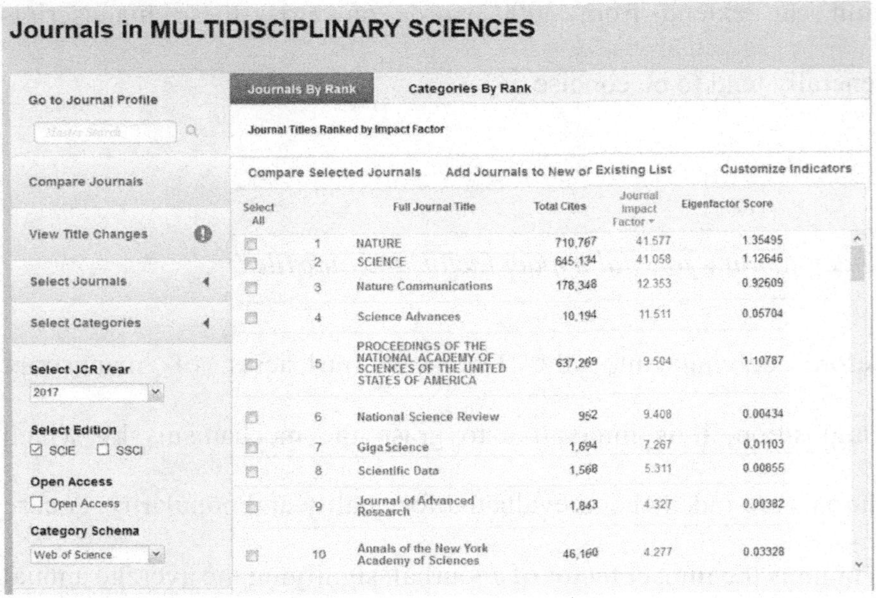

Select All		Full Journal Title	Total Cites	Journal Impact Factor	Eigenfactor Score
	1	NATURE	710,767	41.577	1.35495
	2	SCIENCE	645,134	41.058	1.12646
	3	Nature Communications	178,348	12.353	0.92609
	4	Science Advances	10,194	11.511	0.05704
	5	PROCEEDINGS OF THE NATIONAL ACADEMY OF SCIENCES OF THE UNITED STATES OF AMERICA	637,269	9.504	1.10787
	6	National Science Review	952	9.408	0.00434
	7	GigaScience	1,694	7.267	0.01103
	8	Scientific Data	1,568	5.311	0.00855
	9	Journal of Advanced Research	1,843	4.327	0.00382
	10	Annals of the New York Academy of Sciences	46,160	4.277	0.03328

Figure 5.1 List of Web of Science-indexed journals from the multidisciplinary science field, indicating the journal impact factor and other metrics, such as total cites and Eigenfactor score. Only the top 10 highest-impact journals from this category are displayed (the screenshot was obtained from https://jcr.clarivate.com/ in July 2019).

It is worth noting that alternative indexing bodies, such as Scopus, may adopt distinct methodologies and calculations. For instance, Scopus introduces CiteScore (refer to https://www.elsevier.com/editors-update/story/journal-metrics/citescore-a-new-metric-to-help-you-choose-the-right-journal). Nonetheless, caution is advised, as predatory publishing houses (discussed in detail in Chapter 7) may also index their questionable journals. Therefore, prudence is essential when assessing metrics such as impact factor, especially if they emanate from unverified authorities.

In the realm of contemporary academia, the assessment of journal quality has advanced to include quartiles, denoted as Q1 through Q4. This metric involves the categorization of journals within a specific scientific field into four distinct groups. The top 25% is attributed to Q1 journals, the subsequent 25% to Q2, and so forth, concluding with the lowest 25%, designated as Q4. For instance, in a scenario with 100 journals within a scientific field, the leading 25 journals, ranked based on their impact factors, acquire the status of Q1 journals, while the trailing 25 journals fall under the category of Q4. It is crucial to emphasize that such categorization is diligently carried out by esteemed indexing entities, namely Web of Science and Scopus (refer to Figure 5.2).

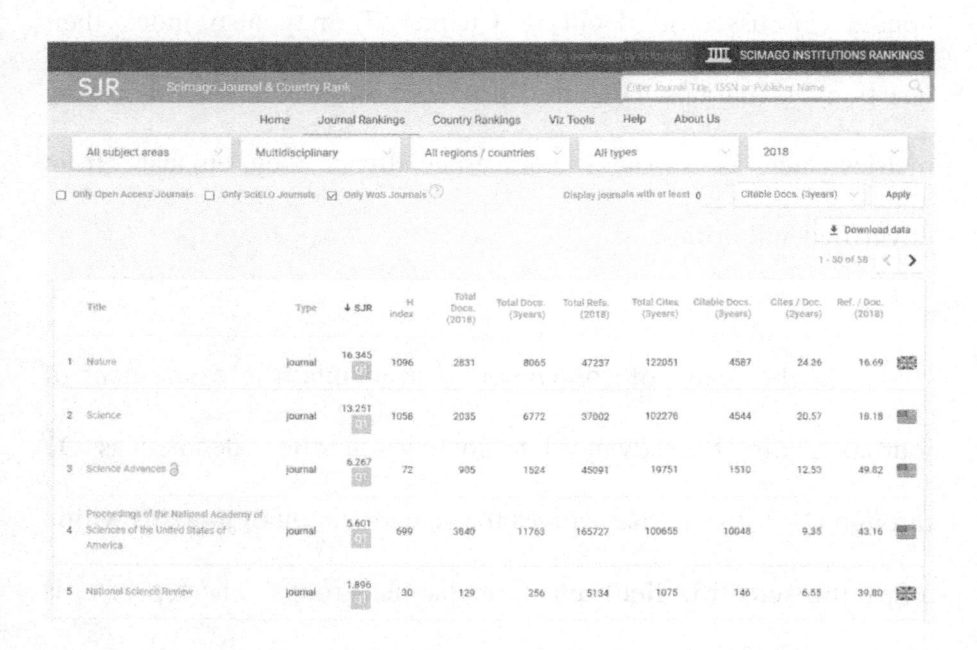

Figure 5.2 Enumerating Scopus-indexed journals within the multidisciplinary domain, we delineate the journal quartiles, focusing

specifically on the top five journals bearing the coveted Q1 rank. Additionally, various metrics, including the H-index and SCImago Journal Rank (SJR), are presented for elucidation. It is pertinent to note that the accompanying screenshot was procured from https://www.scimagojr.com/ in July 2019.

The H-index (named after its inventor, Jorge E. Hirsch) stands as yet another pivotal determinant of quality within academic circles. This metric gauges the excellence of a journal's output in terms of high-quality papers that attract regular citations. The calculation involves initially ranking a journal's manuscripts based on the number of citations they accrue. Subsequently, the H-index is determined by identifying the position where the number of citations is equivalent to the journal number. To exemplify, an H-index of 1 implies that at least one paper has been cited at least once (potentially more, but given the solitary publication, the H-index remains at 1). Conversely, an H-index of 10 indicates that a minimum of 10 papers have each garnered at least 10 citations (or more), and so forth. It is noteworthy that this same metric is employed in computing the H-index for researchers.

Research manuscript arrangement

The structuring of a Type 1 (research) manuscript offers two principal options contingent upon the guidelines provided by the journal, as delineated in Figure 5.3. The first is denominated as AIMeRDisC, representing a more conventional format. In this configuration, the manuscript unfolds sequentially from the abstract to the introduction, methods, results, discussion, and finally, the conclusion. Conversely, the alternative arrangement is referred to as AIRDCoM, where the method section is positioned towards the conclusion of the manuscript, just preceding the reference list. It is imperative to scrutinize and adhere to the specific guidelines stipulated by the target journal.

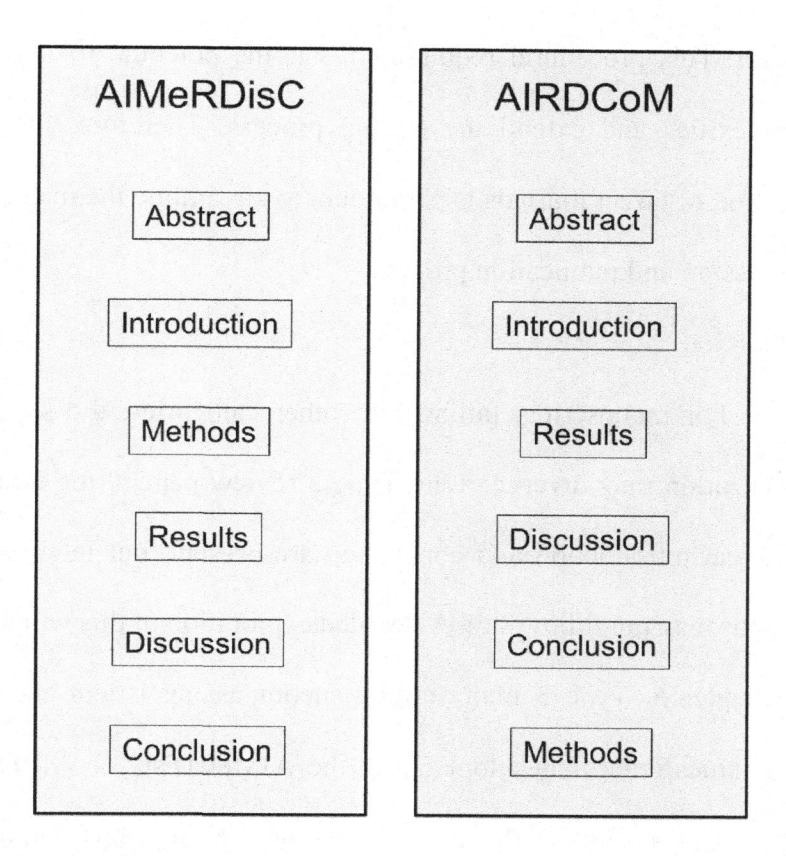

Figure 5.3 Two choices of research manuscript arrangements, AIMeRDisC and AIRDCoM.

A noteworthy point to consider is that in cases where the AIRDCoM arrangement is mandated, it becomes essential to define abbreviations and pertinent methodological details early in the results section. This procedural requirement has the potential to introduce complexities and extend the editing process. Therefore, judicious selection of target journals is paramount to streamline the manuscript submission and publication process.

For manuscripts falling into other categories, the structural organization may diverge. Take Type 2 review papers, for example, where an introduction and conclusion are present, but intermediary sections may not follow suit. A detailed exploration of this will unfold in Chapter 6. Type 3 manuscripts, encompassing letters and short communications, may adopt either the AIMeRDisC or AIRDCoM arrangements, without distinct subsections—though, this could vary across journals. In contrast, Type 4 manuscripts, such as opinion and perspective papers, may assume a more essayistic form without adhering to a discrete structural framework. On the flip side, Type 5 manuscripts, dealing with data and methods, might feature an abstract, introduction, and method sections, potentially lacking extensive results and/or discussion segments.

As expounded in Step 2 of Chapter 4, the writing process can be tailored to individual preferences. To sustain motivation, initiating the writing process with the methods section is recommended—a task deemed more straightforward for most individuals. This progression should align with the figures and tables presented in the manuscript. Subsequently, the Results section, followed by the Introduction, Discussion, and concluding with the Conclusion and Abstract, can be approached in this order. A thorough exploration of each of these sections will be undertaken in the ensuing discussion.

Methods section: the toolbox

The Methods section, quintessentially straightforward in a research manuscript, assumes the role of a toolbox—meticulously outlining the procedures employed in experimentation, thereby providing the essential framework for data presentation in the paper. This meticulous detailing is imperative to enable fellow scientists to grasp the techniques and facilitate replication. Indeed, reputable journals mandate the comprehensive disclosure of all experimental procedures leading to data collection.

In the realm of biology field papers, this section typically commences with either "Materials" or "Experimental Design," culminating in "Statistics." Alignment with the flow of results is crucial, necessitating a thorough consistency check upon the completion of both manuscript sections. As elucidated in Chapter 4, the finalization of figures and tables in collaboration with your supervisor governs the subsequent flow of this method section. For example, if the initial figure features stages or conditions of organisms (be they plants, animals, or microbes), the corresponding subsection in the Methods would appropriately delve into the experimental design.

However, students often encounter challenges in composing this section, owing to intricate workflows with numerous interwoven protocols and methodologies. Another plausible hurdle arises when experiments are conducted by research assistants without proper documentation. Supervisors bear the onus of vigilant oversight over their students and laboratory staff in terms of project management to avert mismanagement pitfalls that may lead to reproducibility issues, squandering time and resources on experiment replication. It is imperative to note that the language employed in this Methods section predominantly adopts a past tense, delineating past experimentation. Additionally, adherence to the International System (SI) units for measurements and metrics in this section is paramount, facilitating global replication of the methods in laboratories worldwide.

Results section: the descriptor

The Results section serves as the pedal for a bicycle, propelling the manuscript's narrative. It functions as the elucidator for the primary figures and tables embedded in our manuscript. Remarkably, it stands as one of the more straightforward chapters to compose, delineating results without delving into interpretation and discussion. This section is subdivided into various headings, succinctly encapsulating the experimental work and guiding readers through the manuscript's narrative. The language employed in the Results section adopts a present tense when describing figures or tables and shifts to the past tense when elucidating findings.

Caution should be exercised to avoid presenting superficial sentences devoid of context, particularly in the case of extensive data figures or tables where numerous aspects necessitate explication. Prioritizing key points germane to the manuscript is advised, with a focus on highlighting significant patterns for a concise explanation. Supervisor feedback is invaluable for refining the writing in this section.

Emphasis must also be placed on finalizing figures and tables with the correct flow, a critical aspect in facilitating the ease of completing this section. The main results should be appropriately described, with brief commentary on overarching themes. While it is crucial to refrain from introducing discussion points in this section, exceptions may arise, justified by the need to explain experimental decisions or anomalies within the data.

Alternatively, the Results section may be integrated with the Discussion section (Result and Discussion section), contingent upon the manuscript's narrative complexity. A straightforward storyline aligns the discussion with the flow of the Results section, correlating with the order of figures and tables. However, a separate Discussion section affords greater flexibility in formulating sentences, enabling critical arguments irrespective of figure/table order.

Introduction section: the prelude

The Introduction section serves as the overture, setting the stage for the forthcoming manuscript. Typically, it elucidates the rationale behind the experiment and elucidates its relevance to the study.

Crucially, key concepts that will be expounded upon in the paper are introduced, catering to readers with varying levels of expertise in the research area. This inclusive approach not only aids comprehension for those outside the immediate field but also facilitates the integration of research or ideas by scientists from diverse backgrounds.

Of paramount importance is the articulation of the "loophole or gap in literature," a critical aspect to underscore the study's significance. This gap, discerned through an exhaustive examination and comparison of extensive reports and articles, serves as the locus where the study's novelty is accentuated. It is noteworthy that within scientific hotbeds like human cancer and diseases, where multiple research laboratories may concurrently engage with the same topic, rapid publication should not serve as a pretext for overlooking the need to justify disparities with previously published work. Citing ignorance of other groups' research is deemed an inadequate rationale.

Furthermore, the Introduction section should expound upon the study's importance, establishing the significance, priority, and timeliness of the reported data and study. This strategic framing aims to captivate readers, compelling them to delve deeper into the manuscript and ultimately cite it.

As a general convention, the Introduction commences with a broad statement and progressively hones in on the study's aim, creating a gradient of focus. This deliberate structuring facilitates a gradual transition from the broad overview of the study to a nuanced concentration on the subject of interest. Language in this section predominantly utilizes present and present participle tenses for commonly known facts, with a shift to past and past participle tenses when discussing previously published papers.

Discussion section: the deliberation

The Discussion section stands out as the most formidable segment of scientific manuscript writing. It entails a meticulous examination of results within the context of the relevant scientific domain. Essentially, this necessitates the integration of obtained results with the existing knowledge in the literature, demanding extensive readings, particularly for elucidating the acquired results.

Within the Discussion section, the criticality and thoughtfulness of the authors come under scrutiny. It is here that the justification of results within the current scientific understanding is expounded upon. This section serves as the main focal point of the entire manuscript, particularly appealing to those seeking a comprehensive understanding of the topic. A common pitfall in this section is the tendency to overstate or excessively extrapolate from the given data. While the Discussion is instrumental for connecting previous data and speculating on future studies, undue extrapolation can veer into speculative realms. Thus, maintaining a realistic interpretation is paramount.

Occasionally, the Discussion may share similarities with the Introduction section. This is because, while the Introduction outlines current literature on a topic, the Discussion may further utilize those papers to construct a broader understanding. These two sections must exhibit coherence, steering clear of redundancy. A meticulous comparison of both sections is imperative to minimize repetition and ensure seamless articulation and comprehensiveness.

In this section, the choice of language style becomes pivotal, as alluded to by Cargill and O'Connor (2009). Author claims within the Discussion can be classified as either strong or weak. A strong claim implies that authors have substantiated the results through multiple experiments, using verbs such as prove, demonstrate, establish, or exhibit. On the other hand, weak claims, employing verbs like suggest, indicate, propose, or show, are typically reserved for results open to further refinement in future experiments. Striking the right balance in the strength of claims is critical for paper acceptance. Overly strong claims lacking a solid foundation may lead to rejection, perceived as "too much exaggeration" by reviewers. Conversely, overly weak claims may cast doubt on the trustworthiness of the results. Hence, a discerning approach to claims within the Discussion is prudent, ensuring clarity without compromising reader understanding.

Conclusion: the endgame

The Conclusion section serves as the culminating segment, consolidating critical points and encapsulating the key takeaway message of the manuscript. It neither contains nor should incorporate new information or citations. Caution is urged against speculation and excessive extrapolation within this section, recognizing its primary function to recapitulate the ideas interwoven in the comprehensive Discussion section. Compact and devoid of extensive discussion, this one-paragraph conclusion should be crafted meticulously, ideally towards the final stages of manuscript writing after all other sections are well-articulated.

Importantly, the Conclusion should refrain from resembling a reiterated Abstract. While both sections share key points, they should not be identical. The fundamental disparity lies in the fact that the Abstract provides a summary of the introduction, method, result, and discussion pertinent to the research paper, while the Conclusion succinctly encapsulates key findings, directly addressing the research question and paving the way for broader inquiries or future studies.

Similarly to the abstract, readers with limited time for perusal may find the Conclusion to be a convenient section for grasping the essence of the entire manuscript. It is noteworthy that certain journals may not explicitly designate a separate section for the Conclusion, incorporating it instead at the end of the Discussion section. Ensuring adherence to the appropriate formatting is imperative when selecting a target journal.

Abstract: the summation

The Abstract stands as one of the final components to be composed in a scientific publication. It encapsulates the essence of the paper, enabling readers to swiftly apprehend the content within the manuscript. Initiating its composition prematurely may lead to substantial revisions later if the writing veers in a different direction than anticipated. The Abstract adheres to a typical structure, commencing with a brief introduction of the topic, delineating the study's necessity, summarizing the methodology, outlining the main results, and encapsulating the key points and take-home messages from the discussion.

While this may appear deceptively simple, students and early-career researchers often grapple with succinctly encapsulating the paper's message within the stringent word limit, typically ranging from 300 to 400 words. It is imperative that the abstract authentically mirrors the study, refraining from excessive extrapolation or hyperbole that may not align with the comprehensive manuscript.

The Abstract, akin to a doorway to the full manuscript, holds the potential to entice busy readers to download and thoroughly peruse our paper. A well-crafted abstract substantially contributes to long-term paper citation. It must accurately convey the overarching messages of the paper, ensuring clarity in explanation. Additionally, introducing key terms employed in the manuscript (distinct from keywords) optimizes search terms, enhancing the likelihood of researchers stumbling upon our article during searches using relevant keywords. This, in turn, attracts a broader readership, further disseminating and promoting our research.

Title: the attraction

While the Title is not formally designated as a section within the manuscript, as previously discussed, a meticulously crafted title stands as the linchpin for a paper's allure. It's safe to assert that a compelling title significantly enhances the visibility of our paper. Typically, time-pressed readers only engage with the initial five words of a title. Consequently, those initial words must pique their interest, prompting them to delve deeper into the remainder of the title. Titles commencing with generic phrases like "Investigation/study of a certain organism" may squander the prime real estate of crucial terms. Instances of articles featuring excessively long titles abound, contributing little to aiding readers in deciphering vital information the authors intend to convey.

Titles should embody directness, clarity, and conciseness to captivate readers' attention. The use of jargon, abbreviations (except for terms widely recognized in the field such as DNA, RNA, etc.), and convoluted sentences should be eschewed. Titles ought to be as straightforward as possible, encapsulating the accurate essence of the paper while remaining comprehensive enough for readers to assimilate. An exemplar of a well-constructed title is presented in Figure 5.4, wherein Bunawan et al. (2011) adeptly employ the first five words to convey significance to the reported study ("Foliar anatomy and micromorphology of..."). They conclude with "... and their taxonomic implications," alluding to a broader discourse within the manuscript. Such titles bring out the best in a manuscript, emphasizing key points while exercising judicious word choice.

Australian Journal of Crop Science   *AJCS*

AJCS 5(2):123-127 (2011)   ISSN:1835-2707

Foliar anatomy and micromorphology of *Polygonum minus* Huds. and their taxonomic implications

Hamidun Bunawan[1], Noraini Talip[2], Normah M. Noor[1,3*]

[1]Institute of Systems Biology, Universiti Kebangsaan Malaysia, 43600 Bangi, Selangor, Malaysia
[2]School of Environmental and Natural Resources Sciences, Faculty of Science and Technology, Universiti Kebangsaan Malaysia, 43600 Bangi, Selangor, Malaysia
[3]School of Biosciences and Biotechnology, Faculty of Science and Technology, Universiti Kebangsaan Malaysia, 43600 Bangi, Selangor, Malaysia

*Corresponding author: normah@ukm.my

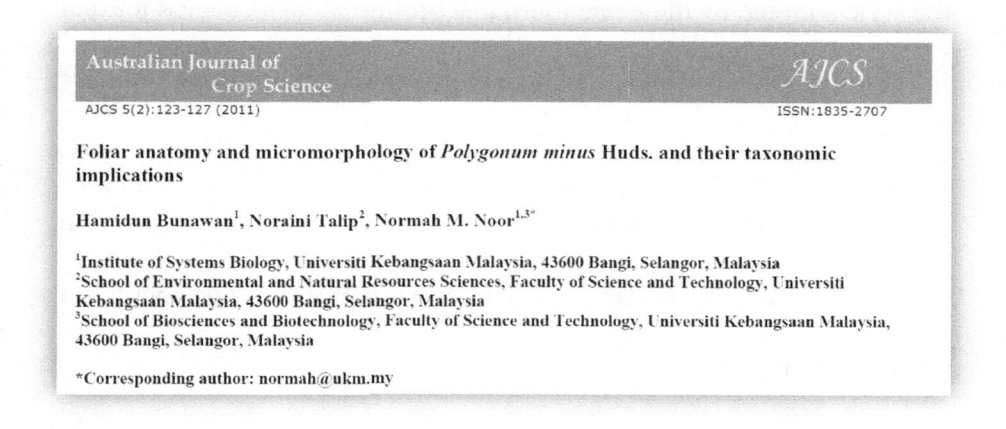

Figure 5.4 An example of an excellent manuscript title by Bunawan et al. (2011). Manuscript front page courtesy of Hamidun Bunawan.

References: the sources

The reference section emerges as arguably the most laborious segment in a paper, serving as the repository of our justifications and supporting arguments. Diverse journals adhere to distinct formatting styles, whether APA, Harvard, or proprietary styles, leading to potential challenges for authors when transitioning a manuscript submission between journals. Figure 5.5 furnishes an illustration of the style adopted by the PeerJ journal, a prominent open access journal in multidisciplinary fields. It underscores the significance of authors meticulously adhering to the specific formatting instructions provided by each journal before submission, as they vary widely. Such attention to detail is imperative to navigate the nuanced requirements of different journals.

> *PeerJ* uses the 'Name. Year' style with an alphabetized reference list.
> In-text citations
> - For three or fewer authors, list all author names *(e.g. Smith, Jones & Johnson, 2004)*. For four or more, abbreviate with 'first author' et al. *(e.g. Smith et al., 2005)*.
> - Multiple references to the same item should be separated with a semicolon (;) and ordered chronologically.
> - References by the same author in the same year should be differentiated by letters *(Smith, 2001a; Smith, 2001b)*.
> - Cite articles accepted for publication as *'in press'*. Include in reference section and upload as a Supplemental file.
> - Cite work unpublished, in preparation or under review as *'unpublished data'*. Supply the author's first initial and surname, and the year of the data collection, in the text citation and do not include the citation in the reference section. Example: (A Castillo, 2000, unpublished data).
> - Avoid referencing personal communications. Reference as *'pers. comm.'*, including the first initial and surname, and year. Example: (A Castillo, 2000, pers. comm.).
>
> The Reference Section
> - Journal reference format: List of authors (with initials). Publication year. Full article title. *Full title of the Journal*, volume: page extents. DOI (if available).

Figure 5.5 The referencing style used by PeerJ. Such details can be obtained from the journal website (https://peerj.com/about/author-instructions/).

Fortunately, numerous tools are at our disposal to facilitate this process. Notably, Endnote (subscription-based) and Mendeley (free) are commonly employed software for referencing. These tools streamline the conversion of citation styles to match prescribed journal formats with just a few clicks. Nonetheless, manual verification remains essential to ensure the accuracy of cited information. Errors may persist if citations are inserted incorrectly, underscoring the importance of meticulous scrutiny in finalizing this section.

While one might perceive the reference section as relatively unimportant—a mere compilation of full bibliographic details—for authors, it assumes paramount significance in the eyes of journal publishers and editors. It stands as the linchpin of the entire manuscript, influencing journal impact factors and rankings in various indexing bodies by virtue of the citations to previous works or reports. Therefore, meticulous referencing establishes the correct linkage to respective papers, aggregating their citations.

Copyeditors of journals play a crucial role in scrutinizing this section (post paper acceptance, during the in-press phase; refer to Chapter 2 for further elucidation). They meticulously ensure that references are arranged in the correct order with accurate information. In practice, instances of manuscript rejection by editors solely based on incorrectly formatted or misinformation in the reference section are infrequent. This is attributed, in part, to the intervention of copyeditors towards the final stages of publication. However, editors may regard certain papers as falling below the journal's quality standards, necessitating resubmission.

Chapter 6 Strategy To Write A Review Manuscript

Exploring the Pros and Cons of Review Papers

Crafting a review paper stands out as a strategic move to enhance citation metrics. Generally, review papers enjoy robust citation rates and are frequently referenced, given their comprehensive coverage of the literature landscape (refer to Table 6.1). Emerging research articles often seek to contextualize their findings within the existing knowledge domain, making the inclusion of references to reviews a standard practice. Furthermore, the opportunity to cite relevant prior work from one's own repertoire extends the reach of those seminal findings to the global community of researchers.

Table 6.1 Advantages and disadvantages of a review article

Advantages	Disadvantages
Increase citation as reviews are well cited	Time consuming to read and understand primary literature
Only based on available literature	Critical argument is needed
No experimentation is needed	Daunting task for a new career researcher

Embarking on the journey of writing a review necessitates an acknowledgment that it can pose a formidable challenge for some. The task demands not only a substantial investment of time in perusing and assimilating an extensive body of literature but, more significantly, in formulating critical arguments derived from these papers. Consequently, strategies to alleviate this process will be expounded upon in this chapter.

Yet another notable advantage of a review article lies in its assessment being exclusively grounded in existing literature. Given the inherent nature of reviews, there is no necessity for experimental work, distinguishing it from original research articles. Consequently, the likelihood of receiving reviewer comments urging the addition or replication of laboratory experiments, a process that could span months, is virtually nonexistent. Moreover, original research articles frequently hinge on the availability of grants, funding, and specialized instrumentation. In contrast, review articles hinge solely on two factors: ideas and synthesis. So, what might impede you from embarking on crafting a review? It is worth noting, however, that a certain level of expertise may be requisite for aiming at top-tier journals.

Before delving into the writing of a review paper, aspiring authors must comprehend that there exist several types of review articles, namely systematic, scoping, and traditional reviews (refer to Figure 6.1). These variations in reviews have distinct objectives and analytical methodologies (which will be expounded upon later), yet all share the commonality of succinctly covering expansive topics or bodies of literature.

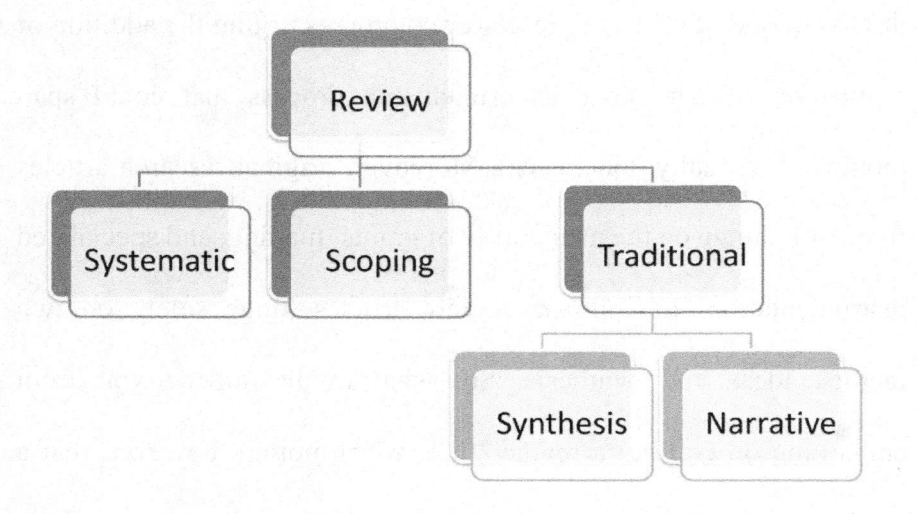

Figure 6.1 The various types of review articles include systematic, scoping, and traditional reviews. The latter, traditional reviews, can be further subdivided into synthesis and narrative reviews.

Systematic review

A systematic review is initially designed to comprehensively assess a specific clinical aspect and healthcare perspective, summarizing evidence derived from reported clinical trials or practices. Its objective is to guide clinicians in determining the most effective treatments or practices for patients within a specific disease context. An illustrative example of such a review is presented in Figure 6.2 below.

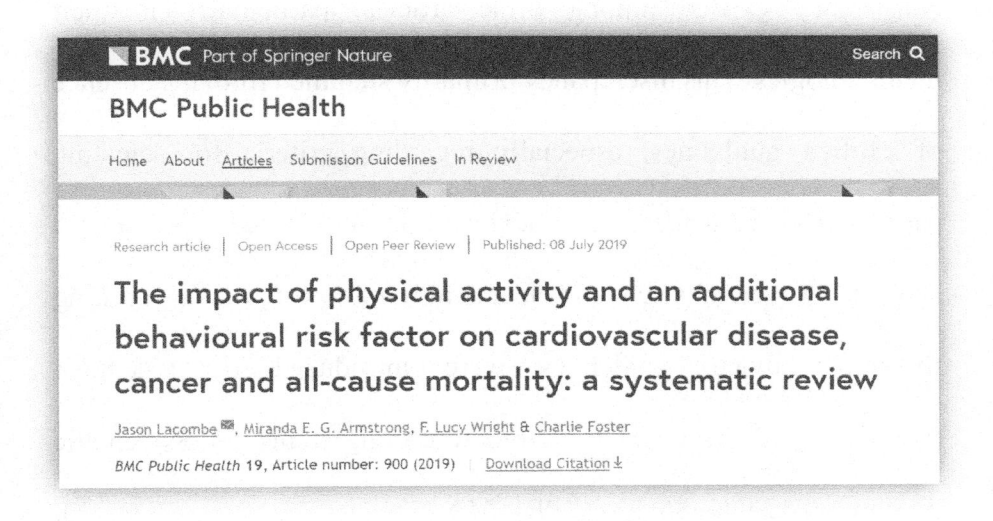

Figure 6.2 An example of a systematic review on childhood obesity intervention (Lacombe et al. 2019). Reproduced with permission under the Creative Commons Attribution 4.0 CC-BY license (https://doi.org/10.1186/s12889-019-7030-8).

In contemporary times, systematic reviews have extended their scope beyond the realm of medicine to encompass diverse fields such as biology and software engineering. Nevertheless, during the initial phases of systematic review development, a notable lack of consistency existed among these articles, particularly in their methodologies. This discrepancy primarily stemmed from the absence of explicit guidelines, especially regarding criteria for selecting papers. Consequently, to address this issue and provide a comprehensive, unbiased, and clear solution for professionals seeking literature advice, guidelines were introduced by Cochrane (www.cochrane.org) and Preferred Reporting Items for Systematic Reviews and Meta-Analyses (PRISMA, http://prisma-statement.org/). PRISMA, in particular, delineates the minimal criteria for reporting such reviews, facilitating a standardized, methodological, and exhaustive approach to the review process. The checklist is presented in Table 6.2 and is accessible on the PRISMA website.

Table 6.2 The PRISMA checklist for writing a systematic review and/or meta-analysis. Reprinted from http://prisma-statement.org/.

Section/topic	#	Checklist item	Page #
TITLE			
Title	1	Identify the report as a systematic review, meta-analysis, or both.	
ABSTRACT			
Structured summary	2	Provide a structured summary including, as applicable: background; objectives; data sources; study eligibility criteria, participants, and interventions; study appraisal and synthesis	

methods; results; limitations; conclusions and implications of key findings; systematic review registration number.

INTRODUCTION

Rationale	3	Describe the rationale for the review in the context of what is already known.
Objectives	4	Provide an explicit statement of questions being addressed with reference to participants, interventions, comparisons, outcomes, and study design (PICOS).

METHODS

Protocol and registration	5	Indicate if a review protocol exists, if and where it can be

		accessed (e.g., Web address), and, if available, provide registration information including registration number.
Eligibility criteria	6	Specify study characteristics (e.g., PICOS, length of follow-up) and report characteristics (e.g., years considered, language, publication status) used as criteria for eligibility, giving rationale.
Information sources	7	Describe all information sources (e.g., databases with dates of coverage, contact with study authors to identify additional studies) in the search and date last searched.
Search	8	Present full electronic search

		strategy for at least one database, including any limits used, such that it could be repeated.
Study selection	9	State the process for selecting studies (i.e., screening, eligibility, included in systematic review, and, if applicable, included in the meta-analysis).
Data collection process	10	Describe method of data extraction from reports (e.g., piloted forms, independently, in duplicate) and any processes for obtaining and confirming data from investigators.
Data items	11	List and define all variables for which data were sought (e.g., PICOS, funding sources) and any

		assumptions and simplifications made.
Risk of bias in individual studies	12	Describe methods used for assessing risk of bias of individual studies (including specification of whether this was done at the study or outcome level), and how this information is to be used in any data synthesis.
Summary measures	13	State the principal summary measures (e.g., risk ratio, difference in means).
Synthesis of results	14	Describe the methods of handling data and combining results of studies, if done, including measures of consistency (e.g., I^2) for each meta-analysis.

Crucially, this checklist serves as a comprehensive guide on how to structure the main sections of the review. For instance, the title must explicitly indicate the nature of the review, whether it's a systematic review, meta-analysis, or both. The abstract provides a summary of the key aspects of the review, while the introduction outlines the rationale and research questions. The method section is pivotal in making a systematic review one of the most descriptive and informative resources for clinical reference. It systematically reviews a topic, identifies databases and search methods, establishes exclusion criteria, and delves into the extent of the research. This meticulous approach results in a well-structured review that comprehensively addresses the research question.

Within the PRISMA workflow (Figure 6.3), several methodological steps are employed to identify and screen potential literature. This ensures the inclusion of all relevant materials while avoiding any oversight that could potentially impact the review's outcome. The workflow begins with the identification of articles from various databases, followed by the removal of redundant duplicates. Full-text eligibility is another inclusion criterion applied before determining the studies included in qualitative and quantitative analyses (Figure 6.3). Authors should engage an independent researcher, preferably a method reviewer (distinct from journal reviewers), to replicate this process. This ensures alignment between authors and reviewers regarding the number and types of manuscripts, facilitating a comprehensive and unbiased review. Moreover, the methodology for journal selection can be registered in PROSPERO (https://www.crd.york.ac.uk/PROSPERO/), allowing for full disclosure of the procedures undertaken during, or preferably before, a systematic review (Figure 6.4).

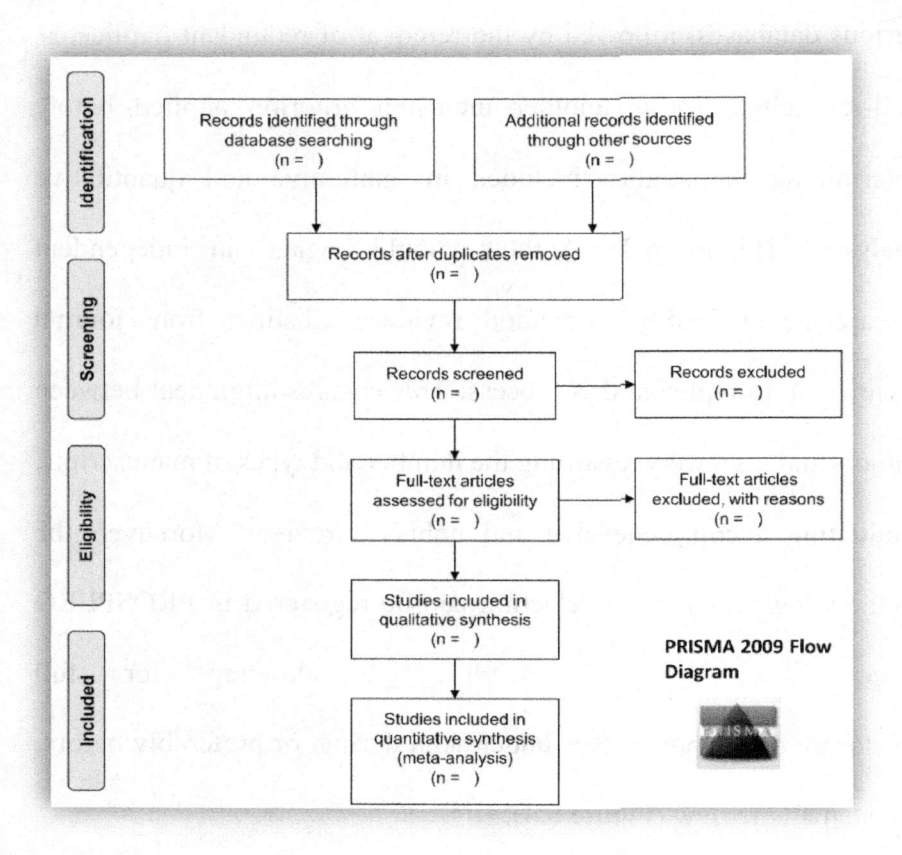

Figure 6.3 The PRISMA workflow for identifying and selecting research papers to be reviewed. Reprinted from http://prisma-statement.org/ (Moher et al. 2009).

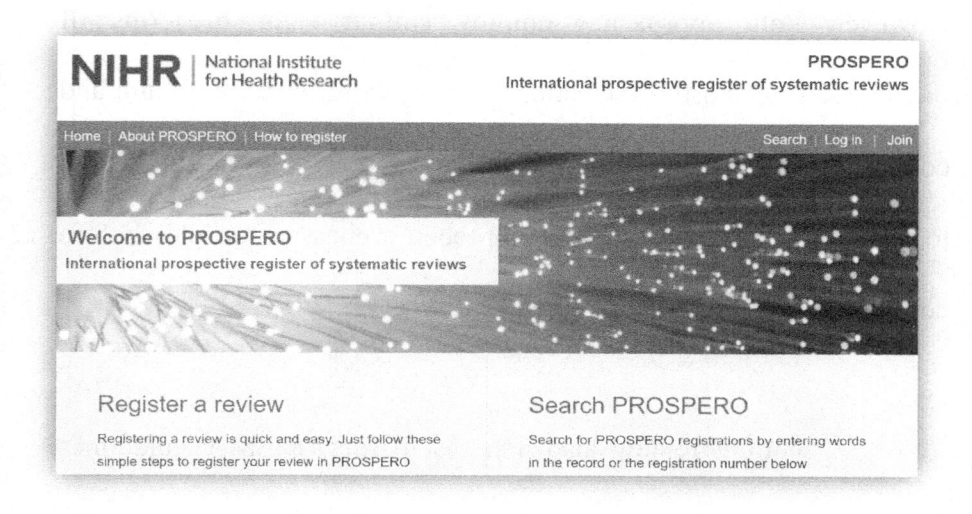

Figure 6.4 Prospero website for registering systematic review protocols (https://www.crd.york.ac.uk/PROSPERO/).

Scoping review

Meanwhile, a scoping review addresses a more expansive research question compared to a systematic review. A scoping review primarily encapsulates a broad body of evidence and primary literature, whereas a systematic review focuses solely on the best articles pertaining to a specific medical topic, especially clinical trials (Pham et al., 2014).

However, both approaches employ similar rigor in terms of methodology and article selection, striving to furnish a thorough and comprehensive review. A scoping review can serve as an initial step to assess the availability and comprehensiveness of articles before committing to a systematic review (Munn et al., 2018).

A scoping review also adheres to the PRISMA guidelines (Table 6.2) to ensure a comprehensive selection of manuscripts. One notable distinction between a systematic review and a scoping review is that the former may involve at least two independent method reviewers to validate the methodology. Additionally, a scoping review does not necessarily need to be registered with PROSPERO, and its methodology is often more straightforward, outlined within the publication itself. An example is provided below (Figure 6.5).

Figure 6.5 An example of a scoping review on various measurements and indicators for maternal and newborn babies (Moller et al., 2018). Reprinted permission is granted under the Creative Commons Attribution 4.0 CC-BY license (https://doi.org/10.1371/journal.pone.0204763).

Traditional review

Another category of review is known as the traditional review. In a traditional review, the scope of the literature search is often not explicitly defined and may vary based on the writers' skills, particularly during the database search. It does not adhere to the conventions followed by systematic and scoping reviews, especially the PRISMA guidelines. This type of review can further be classified into two categories: synthesis and narrative literature reviews.

A synthesis review primarily involves synthesizing the body of literature to construct a cohesive narrative or comprehensive understanding of a specific topic. This approach enables readers to grasp essential aspects within that area of study. On the other hand, a narrative review navigates through all available literature within a given timeframe to provide a comprehensive update on current research trends. The key distinction between a synthesis review and a narrative review lies in the timing of the literature survey. A synthesis review conducts the search for articles after determining the subtopics (Figure 6.6), while a narrative review performs the literature search first before deciding on the subtopics (Figure 6.7).

Respiratory Medicine 122 (2017) 33-42

Contents lists available at ScienceDirect

Respiratory Medicine

journal homepage: www.elsevier.com/locate/rmed

Review article

Beneficial effects of Omalizumab therapy in allergic bronchopulmonary aspergillosis: A synthesis review of published literature

Jian-Xiong Li [a], Li-Chao Fan [a], Man-Hui Li [a, b], Wei-Jun Cao [a, b, 1], Jin-Fu Xu [a, b, *, 1]

[a] Department of Respiratory and Critical Care Medicine, Shanghai Pulmonary Hospital, Tongji University School of Medicine, Shanghai, China
[b] Department of Respiratory and Critical Care Medicine, Shanghai Pulmonary Hospital, Soochow University, Suzhou, China

Contents

1. Introduction 34
2. Methods 34
   2.1. Search strategy 34
   2.2. Selection of studies 34
   2.3. Data management and extraction 34
   2.4. Data analysis 34
3. Results 35
   3.1. Characteristics of included case reports 35
   3.2. Characteristics of the patients included 36
   3.3. Omalizumab dosage 36
4. Evaluation of treatment effects 36
   4.1. Symptom control 36
   4.2. Total IgE change 36
   4.3. Exacerbation 37
   4.4. The change of systemic steroid use 37
   4.5. Lung function test 37
   4.6. Thoracic imaging 38
   4.7. Blood eosinophilia 38
   4.8. Safety 38
5. Discussion 38
6. Conclusion 41
   Funding 41
   Author contributions 41
   Conflict of interest 41
   References 41

Figure 6.6 An example of a synthesis review regarding the benefits of Omalizumab therapy against a specific type of pulmonary infection is presented by Li et al. (2017). In this synthesis review, the main sections encompass the method of analysis and the selection of journal papers. These aspects can be narrowed down and predetermined to shape the content of the review (https://doi.org/10.1016/j.rmed.2016.11.019). Permission to reuse article excerpt is obtained from Elsevier under license number 5751731037737.

> Journal of Advanced Research 20 (2019) 61-70
>
> Contents lists available at ScienceDirect
>
> **Journal of Advanced Research**
>
> journal homepage: www.elsevier.com/locate/jare
>
> Valorization of mangosteen, "The Queen of Fruits," and new advances in postharvest and in food and engineering applications: A review
>
> Wan Mohd Aizat [a,*], Faridda Hannim Ahmad-Hashim [a], Sharifah Nabihah Syed Jaafar [b]
>
> [a] Institute of Systems Biology (INBIOSIS), Universiti Kebangsaan Malaysia (UKM), 43600 Bangi, Selangor, Malaysia
> [b] Bioresource and Biorefinery Laboratory, Faculty of Science and Technology, Universiti Kebangsaan Malaysia (UKM), 43600 Bangi, Selangor, Malaysia

Figure 6.7 An example of a narrative review, which explores mangosteen applications in various studies, is presented by Aizat et al. (2019). In this narrative review, the sections are broad, covering postharvest, food, and engineering applications of this species. Reprinted permission was obtained from Elsevier (https://doi.org/10.1016/j.jare.2019.05.005).

Both synthesis and narrative reviews exhibit their own sets of advantages and disadvantages. For example, a synthesis review proves notably focused, adept at crafting a cohesive narrative to encapsulate a specific topic of interest. However, it may lack breadth in terms of literature coverage, as certain articles might be omitted, either because they did not surface during a targeted literature search or because they are unsuitable for the subtopics addressed in the review paper. Conversely, a narrative review offers more expansive literature coverage, yet the task of formulating a consistent, clear storyline can be formidable. In essence, the distinctions among systematic, scoping, and traditional reviews are succinctly summarized in Table 6.3 below.

Table 6.3 The difference between systematic, scoping and traditional reviews.

Types	Systematic review	Scoping review	Traditional review

Characteristics	Critical appraisal of human trial studies (or other topics)	Wide analysis of human trial studies (or other topics)	Analysis of body of literature
Coverage	Specific	Specific	Broad (can be synthesis or narrative reviews)
Systematic inclusion criteria for literature	Yes	Yes	No
Assessment using PRISMA	Yes	Yes	No
Registration at PROSPERO	Yes	No	No

Independent reviewer for methodology check	Yes	No	No

Review manuscript arrangement

A review manuscript follows a distinct structure compared to regular research articles. Although it includes the customary abstract and introduction, the subdivision of chapters is largely contingent on the author and topic, particularly in the analysis method subsection (as mandated by some journals) and the primary subsections (Figure 6.8). Additionally, it typically concludes with a final remark or future directions, guiding readers towards forthcoming significant works required in that specific topic.

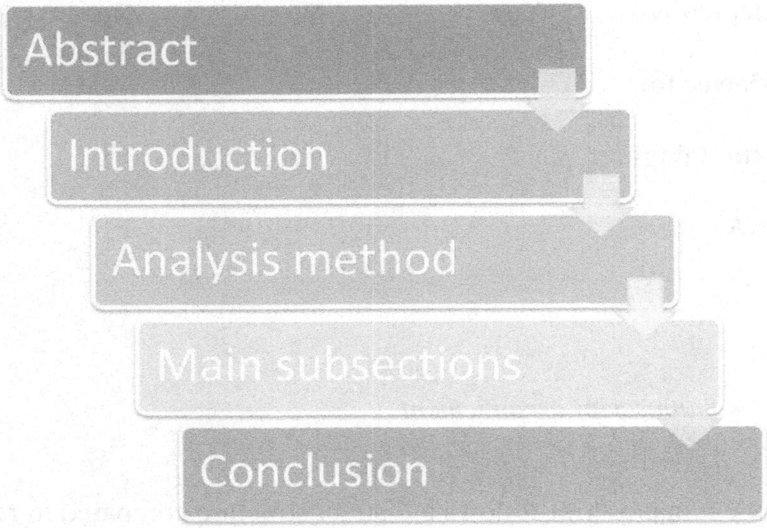
Abstract
Introduction
Analysis method
Main subsections
Conclusion

Figure 6.8 The primary subsections within review articles.

The genre of reviews holds a distinctive position in the realm of science. While primary articles delve into the intricacies of their specific niche areas, review articles curate, synthesize, and critically analyze evidence from numerous research articles, offering a current and comprehensive update. The significance of review articles is underscored by their frequent citations, owing to the substantial amount of work encompassed within these papers.

The structure of a review article is contingent upon the policies of the publishing journal. Some journals may necessitate a survey methodology to validate the inclusivity and exhaustiveness of the incorporated articles. Conversely, journals like PlosOne predominantly seek systematic review articles adhering to the PRISMA guidelines, as discussed earlier. Despite the existence of various review types, including systematic, scoping, and traditional reviews, it is advisable to adopt a methodological survey approach, as elucidated in the subsequent subsection.

A systematic literature search

Conducting a systematic search is imperative for all types of review papers, whether systematic, scoping, synthesis, or narrative. In this subchapter, we will delineate the essential steps to execute a systematic search (Figure 6.9). The process comprises eight steps, encompassing scope determination, database searching, master list generation, thorough examination of papers, and the creation of tables/figures, followed by manuscript structuring, flow checking, formatting, and ultimately submission.

- **Step 1**: Determine scope of study and related KEYWORDS
- **Step 2**: Searching databases and downloading records
- **Step 3**: Systematic and non-redundant master list
- **Step 4**: Paper reading, digesting and making tables/figures
- **Step 5**: Structuring manuscript
- **Step 6**: Reread to determine flow and checking
- **Step 7**: Formatting and obtaining permission
- **Step 8**: Submission and review

Figure 6.9 The eight steps for composing a review article.

The initial step involves authors identifying a suitable, well-balanced topic for review. It is crucial to strike a balance—avoiding the inclusion of an excessive number of manuscripts (more than 200), which would result in an overly broad scope, and steering clear of too few manuscripts (less than approximately 50), indicating insufficient coverage or insignificance for a comprehensive review. The chosen review topic should offer a focus that is both specific and comprehensive, finding the equilibrium between broad and narrow themes.

How does one go about selecting a review topic? Authors often opt for subjects of personal interest, aligning with their specialties or areas of prolonged engagement. This approach provides authors with a distinct advantage in terms of experience and facilitates the discerning selection of relevant journal articles. For students, the choice of a review topic should involve discussions with supervisors, drawing inspiration from ongoing research projects. While this may seem challenging, engaging in conversations with supervisors about potential subtopics within the review can guide students in identifying the most suitable papers for inclusion.

Once a review topic is established, the second step involves database searching. Employing a robust strategy that combines keywords with Boolean operators is imperative for a comprehensive search. The goal is to obtain approximately 200 articles or fewer in each search, ensuring the specificity and relevance of the keywords to the review requirements. An illustrative example is provided from a search conducted in Web of Science (Figure 6.10). The optimal use of Boolean operators is essential and should be accurately entered in the search box. In this instance (Figure 6.10 A), the keyword search is 'swath AND ("data independent acquisition" OR "information independent acquisition")'. This implies that any papers containing the words 'swath' and either 'data independent acquisition' or 'information independent acquisition' will be retrieved. While various search types such as titles, authors, and organizations can be selected with appropriate keywords, the 'topic' type is arguably the most comprehensive, offering extensive coverage of the search keywords.

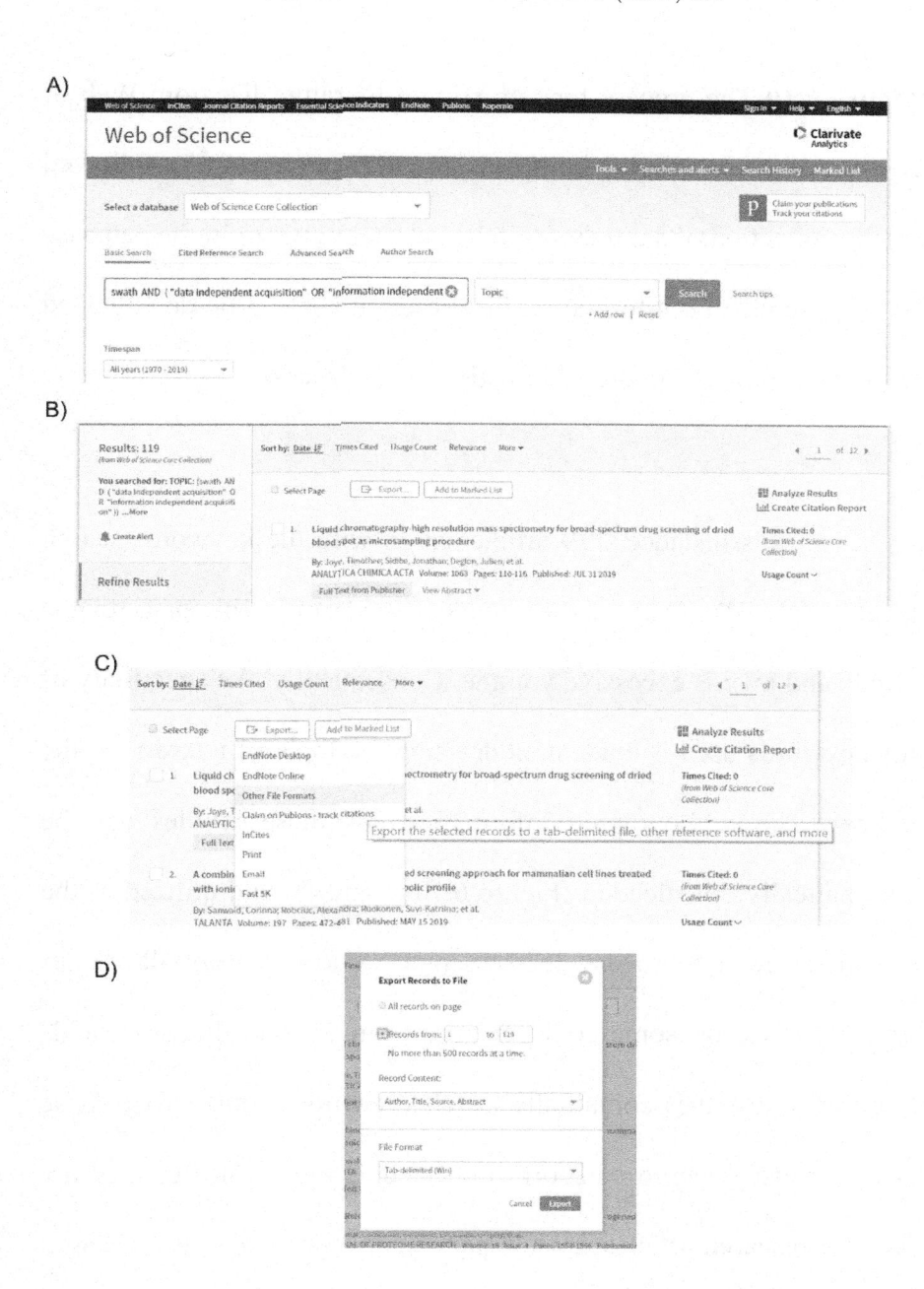

A)

B)

C)

D)

Figure 6.10 The process for retrieving a literature list from Web of Science involves entering keywords into the search box (A), followed by the collection of a number of relevant literatures from the database (B). Subsequently, information for these articles can be downloaded (C and D) to facilitate the systematic review process.

In this instance, 119 articles align with the keywords search (Figure 6.10 B). This number is adequately sufficient for a review article and avoids excessive volume. Consequently, the specificity of the keywords used is evident, addressing the topic of interest for the review. The bibliographic information for these articles can be automatically downloaded (Figure 6.10 C and D) and utilized in the systematic review process. It is essential to note that not all articles may be pertinent; some could emerge from entirely different fields merely because they contain the search keywords. Additionally, these articles must undergo categorization to determine whether they are primary research articles, review papers, or other types, as discussed earlier.

Similarly, keyword-based searching can be conducted in another database, namely Scopus. Utilizing the same keywords employed in the Web of Science search, this yields 101 retrieved articles (Figure 6.11 A). It is essential to acknowledge the potential redundancy with the earlier Web of Science search, necessitating a further filtering process. The information for these Scopus articles must be initially downloaded, as illustrated in Figure 6.11 B, C and D. Additional databases, such as Google Scholar, ScienceDirect, PubMed, and EbscoHost, are also viable for this search process. Authors have the flexibility to explore and apply analogous strategies, as elucidated earlier, to compile the list of papers from these alternative databases.

SCIENTIFIC ARTICLE WRITING (SAW) 101

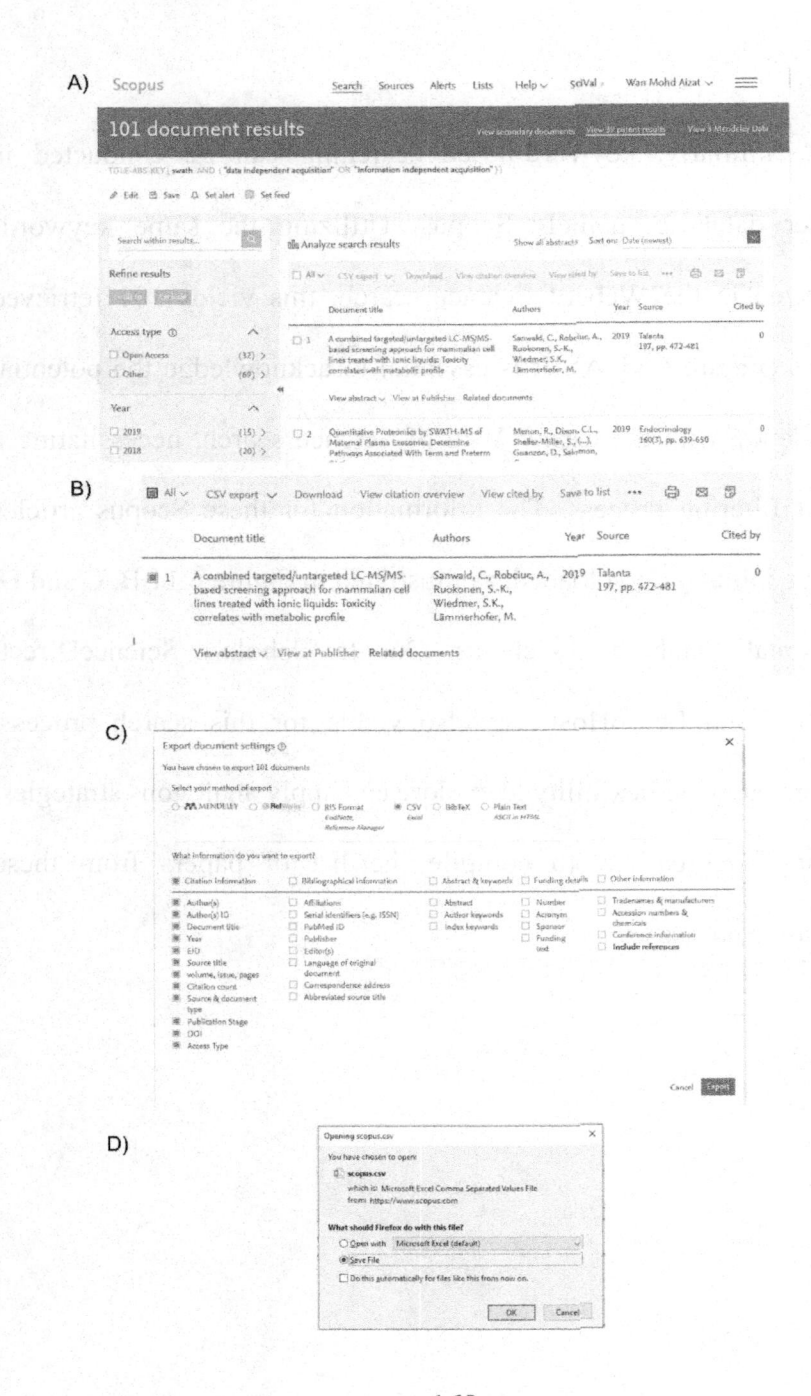

A)

B)

C)

D)

Figure 6.11 The steps for retrieving a literature list from the Scopus database involve searching for keywords (A), resulting in the collection of a number of relevant literatures from the database (B). The information for these articles can then be downloaded (C and D) for use in a systematic review process.

During the quest for articles in databases, several considerations deserve attention. Firstly, the date of access holds significance as it delineates the temporal scope of our review. Secondly, one must ascertain the existence of prior review papers on the chosen topics. If such reviews exist, evaluating their timeliness, especially if they are more than three years old, is imperative and may warrant the creation of a new review article. These inquiries are pivotal in establishing the relevance and contemporaneity of our review. However, should a recent publication cover the exact topic under consideration, it is advisable to slightly alter the focus, ensuring a novel perspective compared to preceding review papers.

The third step involves generating a non-redundant list of article entries through the integration of data from the search databases. To achieve this integration, the downloaded information must be opened and saved in the same Excel workbook but in different sheets. It is crucial to ensure that these distinct databases do not contain any redundant entries within themselves, and this can be achieved through methods such as Conditional Formatting (highlighting duplicate values) or using the Remove Duplicate function. Subsequently, these two sheets are transformed into functional tables using the Ctrl + T function (Figure 6.12 A and B).

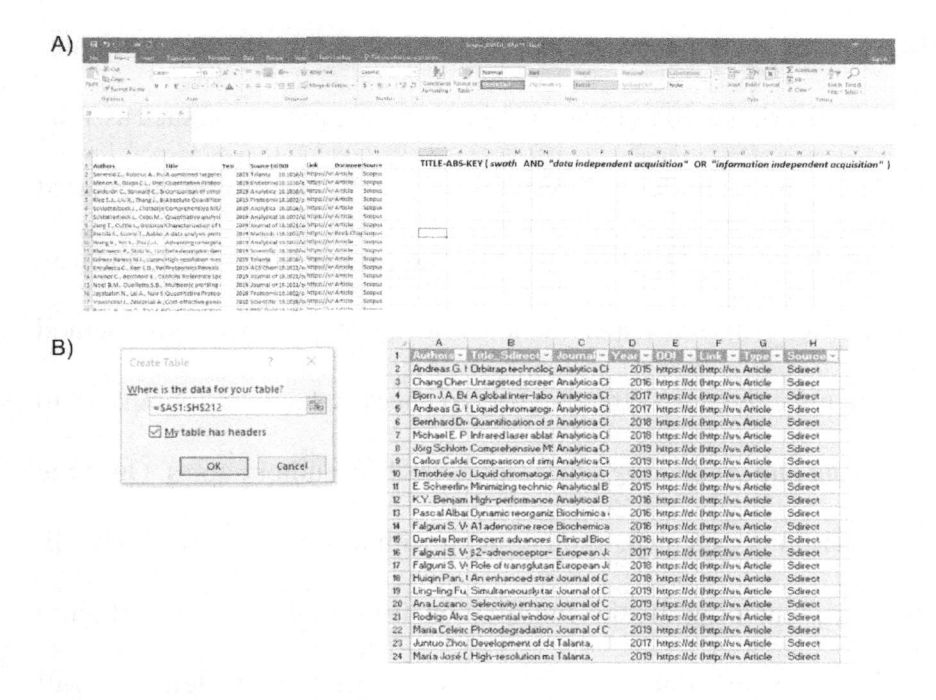

Figure 6.12 Converting an excel sheet (A) into a functional table (B).

Subsequently, a new sheet must be created and named "Nonredundant." On this sheet, the fuzzy lookup function (this Excel add-on can be downloaded for free) is initiated (Figure 6.13 A). The parameter settings window will appear (Figure 6.13 B), and the left and right tables need to be defined—the table with the most entries (having the most papers) as the left table and the second-most entry table as the right table (Figure 6.13 B). Other parameters, such as Title vs Title, and a similarity threshold set to 0.9, need to be configured before clicking "GO." The Title vs Title comparison aims to identify similarities between paper titles. From my experience, this method proves to be the most effective way to check redundancy compared to matching and comparing other values such as author names. Once the comparison is executed, another table with a similarity threshold will appear, containing all the information from both databases (Figure 6.13 C). It is important to note that only entries from the left table will appear, and the right table will display only the entries similar to those in the left table.

Figure 6.13 How to find similar entries from two different databases. A) Fuzzy lookup icon, B) Fuzzy lookup settings, C) Similar entries between two databases have similarity above 0.9.

To eradicate redundancy and guarantee the comprehensive compilation of information from the right table, remove the similar entries from both databases in the "Nonredundant" sheet. Subsequently, copy and paste all entries from the right table (the original list of entries) into the "Nonredundant" sheet, culminating in a thorough and exhaustive table. This procedure can be iterated for other downloaded databases, amalgamating them in a comparable fashion.

Please be aware that certain databases, such as Science Direct, present challenges in data organization. Unlike having entry values such as author names and titles in distinct columns, these databases arrange them in rows, adding complexity to their analysis (Figure 6.14 A). In such cases, it becomes necessary to utilize Notepad++ (https://notepad-plus-plus.org/) to reorganize the entries systematically. Initially, all spaces (denoted as 'CR') should be removed by selecting all entries (Ctrl + A) and replacing space "\r" with "}". Subsequently, eliminate all new line breaks (denoted as LF) by replacing "\n" with " " (none). Identify a common criterion present in all entries that can be used to separate references into different rows. In this case, the word "Keywords" serves this purpose, and we replace all instances with "\nkeywords]" (Figure 6.14 B). Copy and paste the entire table into an Excel sheet (Figure 6.14 C). At this point, you'll observe that the entries are separated into different rows, but the elements (author names, titles, etc.) are not well-segregated into columns. Therefore, the "convert text to column" function (Figure 6.14 D) must be employed. Replace a common symbol (for instance, "}") inserted in the initial step using Notepad++ with different columns (Figure 6.14 E). Finally, inspect the Excel sheet (Figure 6.14 F) to ensure that all entries are correctly in place. This organized data can then be used for matching with different databases, as detailed earlier in Figure 6.13.

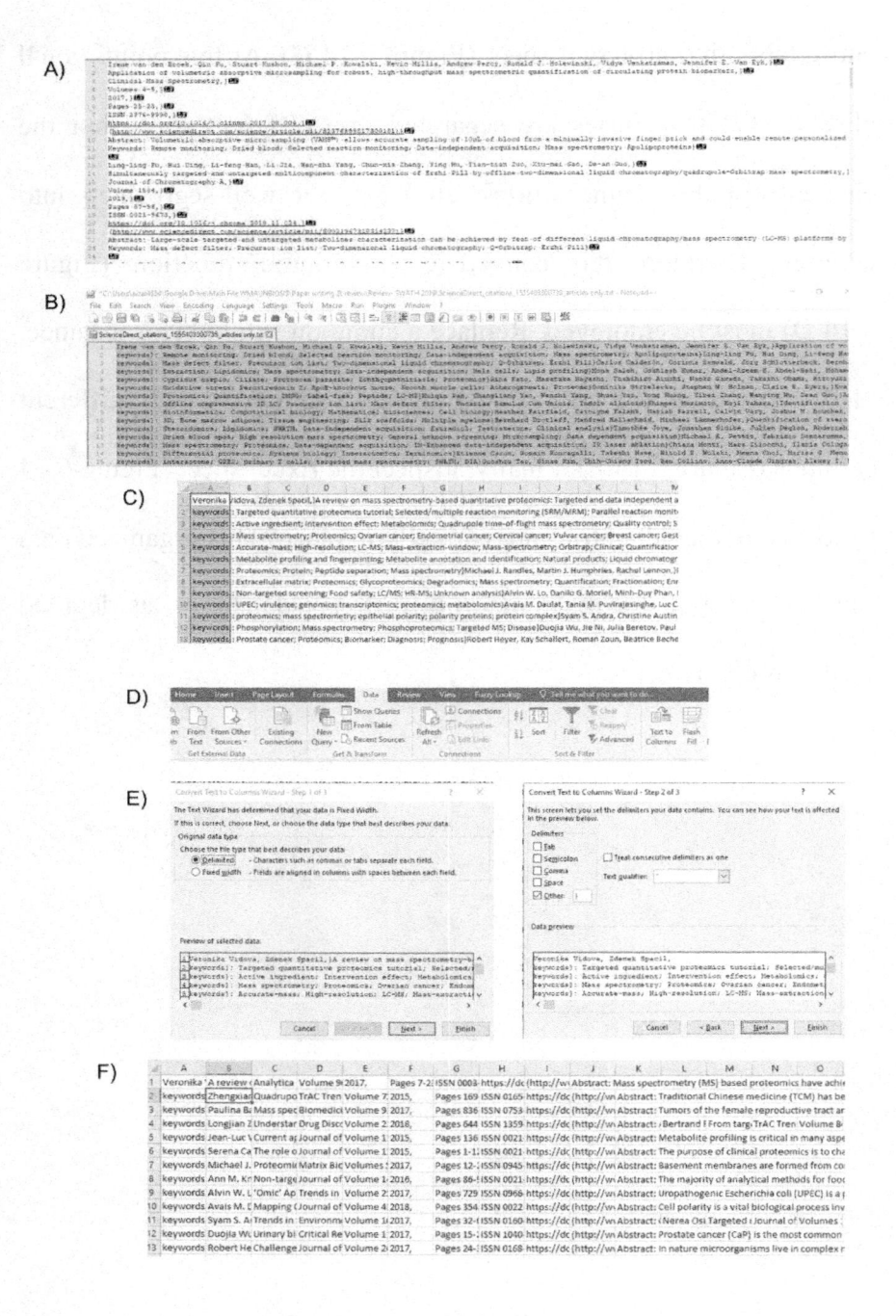

A)

B)

C)

D)

E)

F)

Figure 6.14 The downloaded list from certain databases, such as Science Direct, requires a pre-processing step using Notepad++ and Excel. The text file downloaded must first be opened in Notepad++ (A) before spaces are removed, and "keywords" are aligned (B). Then, the list can be pasted into Excel (C) before being converted to text columns (D and E). The resulting list will consist of a data table with separating columns between the elements.

Once all the articles are compiled, the next step (Step 4) can be initiated. This is where the articles in our "nonredundant" list are critically read and digested to form a table or figure. Normally, I would conduct this in two different phases. The first phase reading is a skim read, classifying themes of different papers. Such themes must align with our earlier decided topic. For example, if our review aims to critically evaluate the applications of a particular technique, then our theme will be the various applications. In this case, we should try to assemble as many articles as possible under one application or another. This will build a repertoire of articles most relevant to that particular application, easing our review process later. If our review is about disease treatments, then our selected themes should be the diverse treatments available for that disease, and so on. Having some focus on where to read will prove beneficial, especially with the hundreds of articles. Also, this is the phase where articles not relevant to the study are removed or marked as such. By this time, the columns in the 'non-redundant' list should be utilized to summarize the themes of those papers.

The second phase of reading is what I call content reading. This phase is about understanding and comprehension so that we know what we write and avoid plagiarism. Incomplete understanding of any article can be dangerous, as it may lead to misleading arguments and false accusations. Given that in the first phase, we have collected similar thematic articles together, we should aim to read to that effect. This will save us time, rather than having to deeply immerse ourselves in each and every sentence. Then, the main outcomes of the study should be concisely summarized in our words, leading to paragraphs of similar article themes. At this time, the written outcomes from those papers may still not be coherent and flow nicely. This is fine because we will consider the flow in the following stages.

Once all the articles relevant to our review are summarized, the next stage (Step 5) is structuring. Why must we do this process before checking the flow? This is because, upon our second phase of reading, it is possible that some of our articles that congregated together in a certain theme may not be pertinent to that topic. This is only realized when we have a deeper understanding of the paper, and our first phase reading may not detect this. Hence, we need to move sentences around to fit our specific needs or take-home messages. In this step, we should also finalize the sub-headings of our articles.

Then, Step 6 is about flow. This is the time when coherency between sentences must be checked within one paragraph or between paragraphs. This step may be done together with the previous step of restructuring. Some sentences not fitting within a certain scope can be reassigned and repurposed accordingly. By this time, a proper review paper should have been constructed.

The next step (Step 7) is formatting and obtaining permission for reused figures. Of course, a target journal should be decided using our earlier strategies (Chapter 2). For figures that might contain copyright items, permissions must be applied through the journal websites, as will be detailed in Chapter 7- Copyright. Finally is the submission step. This has been detailed in Chapter 4- Step 10.

Chapter 7 Ethics in publications

Authorship

Ethics is, perhaps, one of the most formidable terms in science, yet it remains an enigmatic component in research. Ethics permeate and influence all facets of science, transcending across all levels of research and spanning diverse fields. However, even the most seasoned scientists can succumb to ethical concerns, particularly in the realm of publication. Perhaps one of the most contentious ethical issues in various forms of publication, including scientific writing and books, is authorship.

As publication becomes more pivotal than ever in establishing scientific credibility, an increasing number of authors find themselves included in a single paper. However, a clear distinction exists regarding who should be named as authors. One of the widely used guidelines for authorship is outlined by the International Committee of Medical Journal Editors (ICMJE) (Figure 7.1). According to this guideline, individuals entitled to be named as authors must make significant contributions to the project's design, initiation, or direct involvement in activities contributing to the project's completion, including analysis and interpretation. Subsequently, named authors must be engaged in writing, whether at the draft stage or in revisions for the final form. Moreover, authors must provide full consent for the final manuscript to appear in publication. Lastly, authors must confirm the accuracy of all published work and be accountable for any part of it. Meeting all four of these criteria in full (not partially) is a prerequisite for eligibility as authors.

- **Authorship**

  ICMJE INTERNATIONAL COMMITTEE of MEDICAL JOURNAL EDITORS

  1. "Substantial contributions to the conception or design of the work; or the acquisition, analysis, or interpretation of data for the work; AND
  2. Drafting the work or revising it critically for important intellectual content; AND
  3. Final approval of the version to be published; AND
  4. Agreement to be accountable for all aspects of the work in ensuring that questions related to the accuracy or integrity of any part of the work are appropriately investigated and resolved."

Figure 7.1 The guidelines of the International Committee of Medical Journal of Editors (ICJME) on authorship. Statement reprinted from http://www.icmje.org/.

On the flip side, the ICJME provides specific instances where an individual may not qualify for authorship on an article, even if they have some association with the project (Figure 7.2). Firstly, if the person is solely engaged in providing general guidance, managing human resources, or contributing funding. Secondly, if the person is merely overseeing or managing a research group or institution in a general capacity. Lastly, if the individual is only participating in the writing and proofreading processes. Naturally, if any of these individuals make a substantial contribution to the project as outlined earlier, they can be rightfully acknowledged as authors.

> **Do not qualify authorship but acknowledge them..**
>
> **ICMJE** INTERNATIONAL COMMITTEE of MEDICAL JOURNAL EDITORS
>
> 1. "Acquisition of funding, technical advice and personnel
> 2. General supervision of a research group or general administrative support
> 3. Writing assistance, technical editing, language editing, and proofreading"

Figure 7.2 The guidelines of the International Committee of Medical Journal Editors (ICJME) on individuals who should NOT be considered authors but can be acknowledged. Statement reprinted from http://www.icmje.org/.

For individuals who have contributed to the project but do not meet the eligibility criteria outlined by the ICJME guidelines, their acknowledgment can be appropriately made in the acknowledgment section. This section is crucial not only for recognizing the efforts of those who assisted in the project but also for explicitly mentioning any financial support received from grant providers, as this may be a stipulation on their part. An illustrative example of a typical acknowledgment section is presented in Figure 7.3.

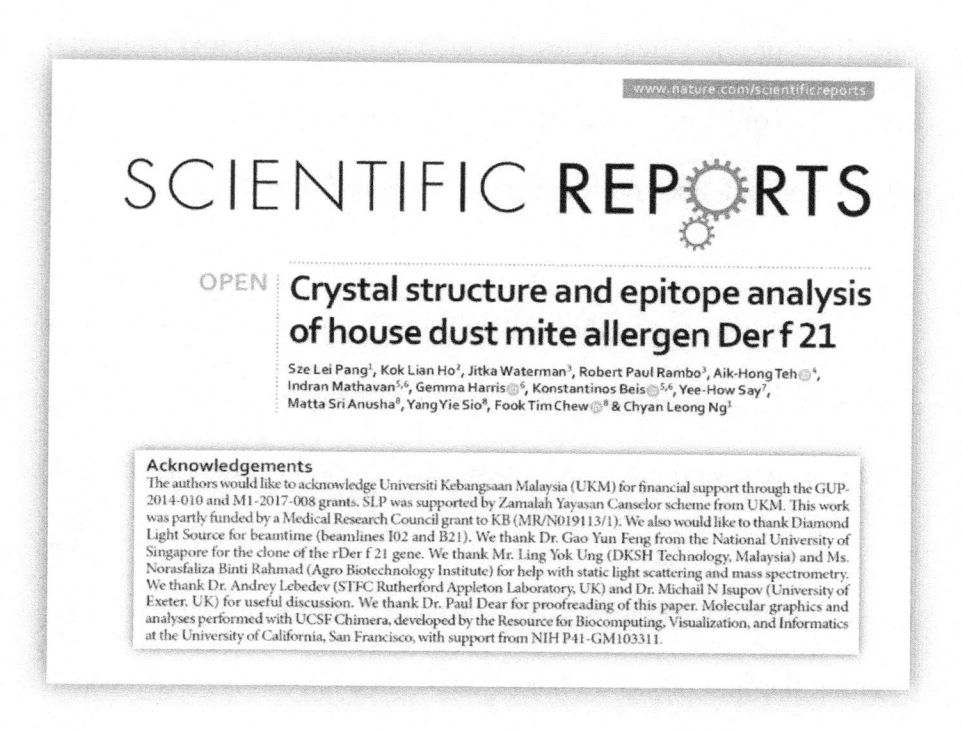

Figure 7.3 A typical acknowledgement section from a publication (Pang et al., 2019). Reprinted with permission under the Creative Commons Attribution 4.0 CC-BY license (https://www.nature.com/articles/s41598-019-40879-x).

The order of authorship can sometimes be a subject of debate, especially regarding who should occupy the first and last positions, as these are considered the most crucial positions in the list. The ICJME guidelines provide clear roles for each author position (Figure 7.4). Regardless of their order, all authors must adhere to the ICMJE authorship guidelines outlined earlier (Figure 7.1 and Figure 7.2).

The primary author of a paper, typically listed first, is responsible for conducting the majority of experiments, whether in wet or dry lab settings. On the other hand, the last author, often the principal supervisor, plays a crucial role in verifying the authenticity and accuracy of the reported data. The corresponding author, who may be either the first or last author (though not exclusively), serves as the primary communicator among all authors, ensuring that everyone is well-informed about the manuscript's content and authorship. Additionally, the corresponding author acts as the main point of contact for journal editors, publishers, and readers.

Authorship responsibilities

First author
- Satisfies all ICJME guidelines
- Most contribution towards the reported study

Middle authors
- Satisfy all ICJME guidelines
- Arrange according to their contribution

Final author
- Satisfies all ICJME guidelines
- Responsible for the accuracy of methodology, analysis and reporting

Corresponding author
- Satisfies all ICJME guidelines
- The middle person to communicate between co-authors, editors, publishers and readers

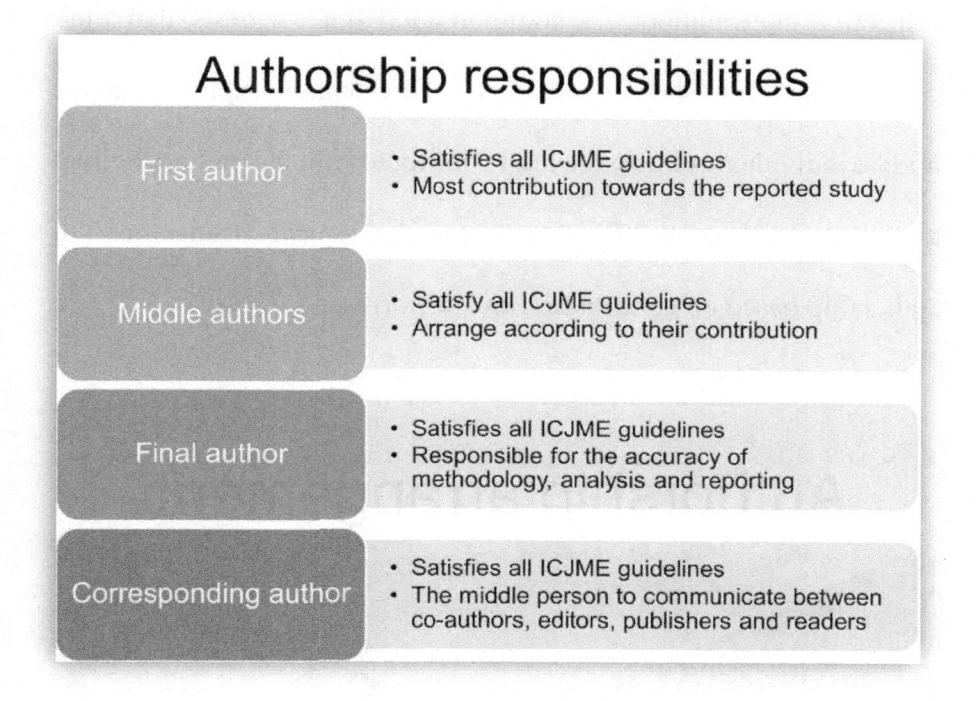

Figure 7.4 International Committee of Medical Journal Editors (ICMJE) guidelines for authorship arrangement (http://www.icmje.org/).

On the contrary, individuals occupying intermediate positions in the authorship hierarchy do not fit into the primary and senior authorship roles outlined earlier; their sequence is determined by their respective contributions. A common guideline suggests that their contribution diminishes from the first or final author, implying that the middle individual is likely the least contributor (though not negligible) to the study. Figure 7.5 encapsulates the typical arrangement of authorship based on contribution and seniority.

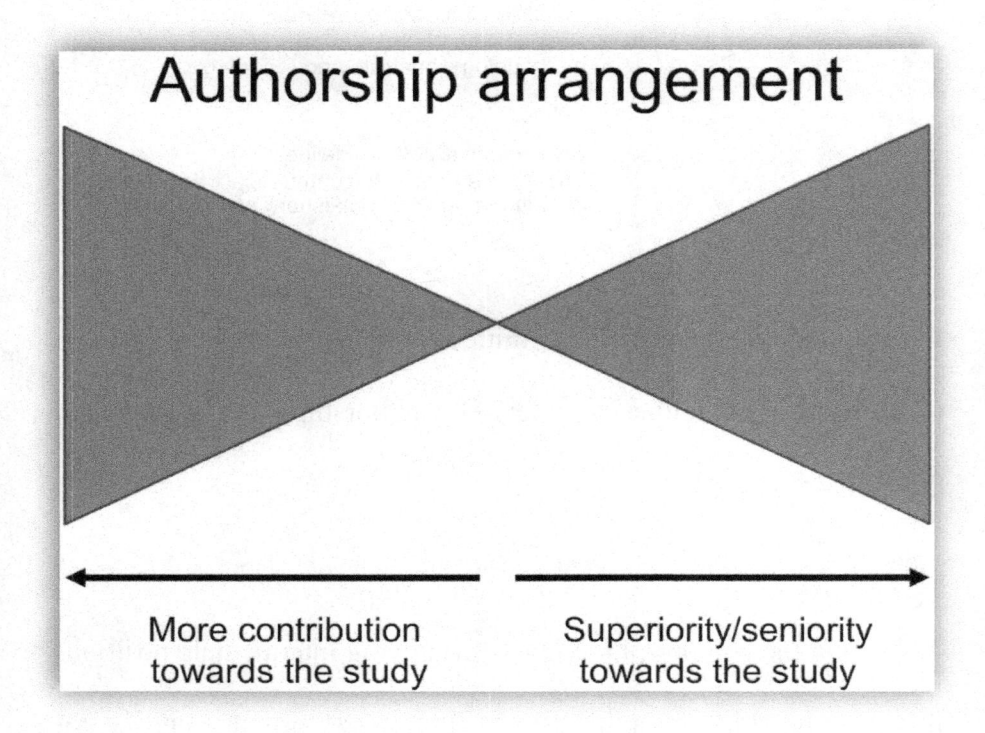

Authorship arrangement

← More contribution towards the study | Superiority/seniority towards the study →

Figure 7.5 The arrangement of authors can be contingent on their contributions and seniority in the project. Nevertheless, all authors must meet the conditions stipulated by the International Committee of Medical Journal Editors (ICJME).

Nonetheless, there are situations in which author contributions and, consequently, the order of authorship can become a significant concern. In a recent incident (Figure 7.6), a postdoctoral fellow at a research centre in New Jersey found herself compelled to share the first authorship position (with her name listed second) in a paper submitted to Nature. Despite her assertion that the majority of the work was carried out by her and not the designated first author, she was terminated from her position and is currently pursuing justice in this matter. This incident underscores that authorship is not a trivial matter and should be approached with transparency and careful negotiation.

Figure 7.6 The recent news highlights problems arising from the order of authorship in a publication. The scientist faced termination for asserting her right to be the first author on a submitted paper. The complete article is available at https://www.sciencemag.org/news/2018/10/was-cancer-scientist-fired-challenging-lab-chief-over-authorship. Reproduction

permission has been authorized by the publisher (Science Journals/AAAS).

On the flip side, various labels have emerged to characterize certain 'unique' authorship practices (Figure 7.7). These include ghost, guest, given, and fake authorship. Firstly, a ghost author is an individual who authors a manuscript but is not acknowledged in the author list. This practice is commonly observed in clinical trials, where companies with noteworthy results often hire external writers (distinct from the scientists conducting the experiments) to draft the papers. Referring back to the ICJME guideline (Figure 7.1), these writers fail to meet all four criteria listed, particularly contributing to the project's conception, progress, and analysis. Consequently, these writers are often excluded from the manuscript, although there is a growing effort to acknowledge them in the acknowledgment section.

Figure 7.7 The different labels associated with various authorship practices.

In the realm of authorship practices, guest and given authorship refer to individuals who, technically unqualified to be authors, are added to a paper for various reasons, such as political influence or funding. Politically, individuals may be included based on their institutional position or post. Additionally, those with influence in a particular research area may be added to enhance the manuscript's perceived reliability. Moreover, individuals may be included due to their funding roles, although this practice typically belongs in the acknowledgement section.

Recently, a new form of authorship malpractice, known as fake authorship (https://doi.org/10.1016/j.trechm.2019.02.005), has emerged. As the name implies, it involves falsifying author names to be included in the author list. Several motivations drive this practice. Firstly, the act of faking names, especially those impersonating well-known scientists, aims to lend credibility to the submitted paper, potentially increasing its chances of acceptance due to the endorsement of a "prominent" scientist. Another reason for fake authorship is to establish a prestigious "collaboration" with world-class institutions. These fabricated authors, often non-existent, are affiliated with institutions possessing various facilities and credentials, creating an appearance of legitimacy that may facilitate successful publication without raising suspicion from editors and reviewers.

Additionally, faking author names may be driven by the desire to present a collaborative team effort. Given that contemporary research is often a collaborative endeavor, the inclusion of fake authors can create the impression of a more extensive team working on the reported findings. Regardless of the motivation behind such practices, they warrant thorough investigation and eradication. The recent implementation of author contribution statements aims to address and prevent wrongful authorship practices (Figure 7.8).

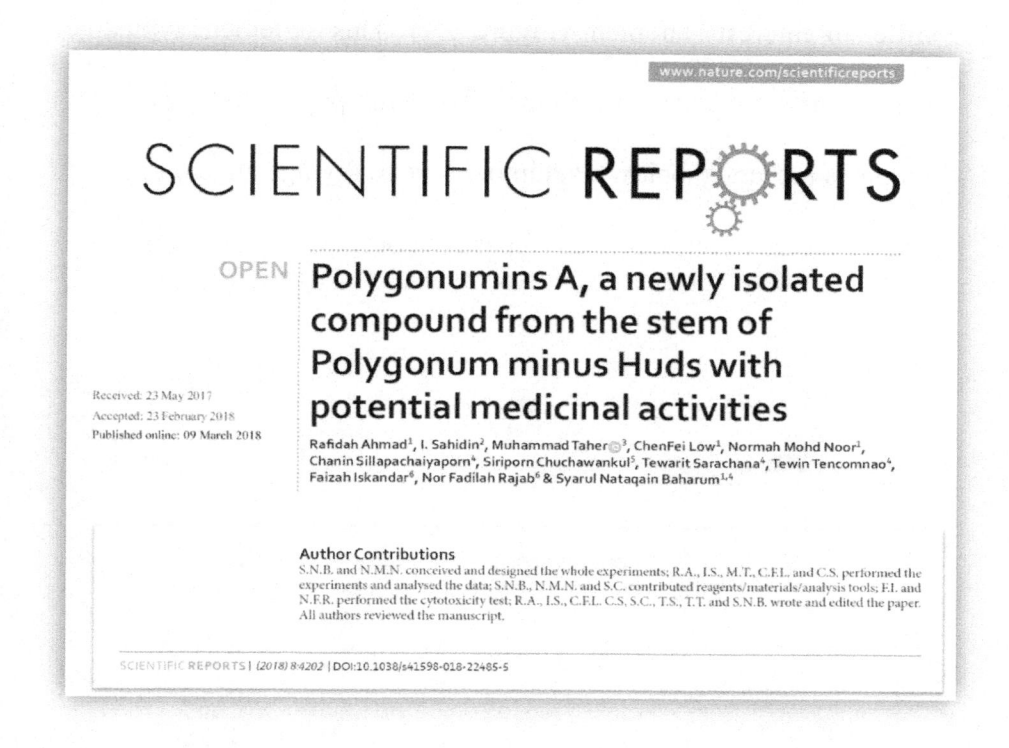

Figure 7.8 The author contribution statement example is drawn from Ahmad et al. (2018), typically positioned near the end of the manuscript. Reprinted permission is granted under the Creative Commons Attribution 4.0 CC-BY license (https://www.nature.com/articles/s41598-018-22485-5).

A method to explicitly disavow any potential influence from funding agencies and collaborators on our manuscript is to draft a conflict of interest statement (Figure 7.9). This statement typically finds placement towards the conclusion of the paper. An illustrative example is presented below. It is imperative to divulge any competing interests, thereby facilitating an impartial assertion by the authors.

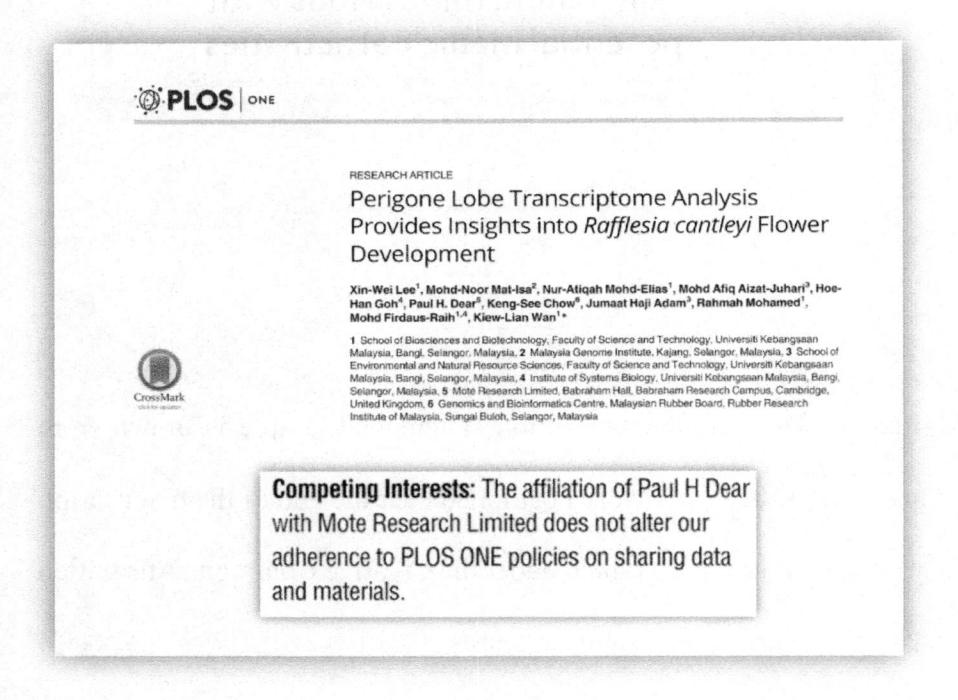

Figure 7.9 A declaration of competing interests can be included in articles to elucidate any external influences (if present) on the presented findings. Reprinted with permission under the Creative

Commons Attribution 4.0 CC-BY license (https://journals.plos.org/plosone/article?id=10.1371/journal.pone.0167958).

Plagiarism

Plagiarism poses another ethical concern within academic writing. It entails the act of replicating statements or works from others without appropriate acknowledgment (Cargill and Connor, 2009). Four distinct types of plagiarism exist, namely direct, self, mosaic, and accidental (https://www.bowdoin.edu/dean-of-students/conduct-review-board/academic-honesty-and-plagiarism/common-types-of-plagiarism.html) (Figure 7.10). Direct plagiarism involves a complete and unattributed reproduction of someone else's work, devoid of citations or quotation marks. Self-plagiarism occurs when one uses their own work in multiple submissions, such as for different journals. Mosaic plagiarism involves minimally altering statements from other authors while preserving their original structure; even if appropriately cited, this form of plagiarism is still considered unethical. Lastly, accidental plagiarism occurs when, despite paraphrasing an entire statement, the original author's idea or work is not properly cited, often unintentionally.

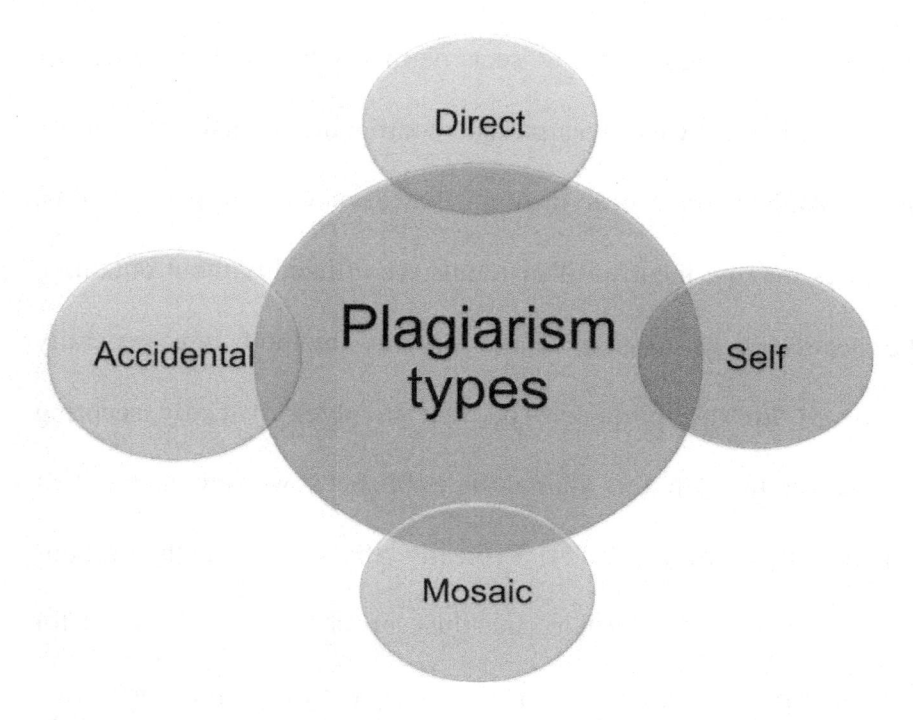

Figure 7.10 The four types of plagiarism are as follows: direct, self, mosaic, and accidental (https://www.bowdoin.edu/dean-of-students/conduct-review-board/academic-honesty-and-plagiarism/common-types-of-plagiarism.html)

Copyright

Materials protected by copyright are derived from published content, including books, journal publications, or publicly available online materials. It is imperative to seek permission before utilizing the content, whether it involves partial modification or using the entire figure. Authors must bear in mind that even with proper citations, penalties may be incurred if materials are utilized without obtaining the necessary permission. Three primary methods are generally employed for this purpose. The first involves officially securing permission through the journal or publisher's website using their online system (Figure 7.11). Typically, the original author retains certain rights to their article, and thus, no charges are incurred for obtaining permission. However, if the request for permission comes from someone other than the original author, charges may be levied before granting permission.

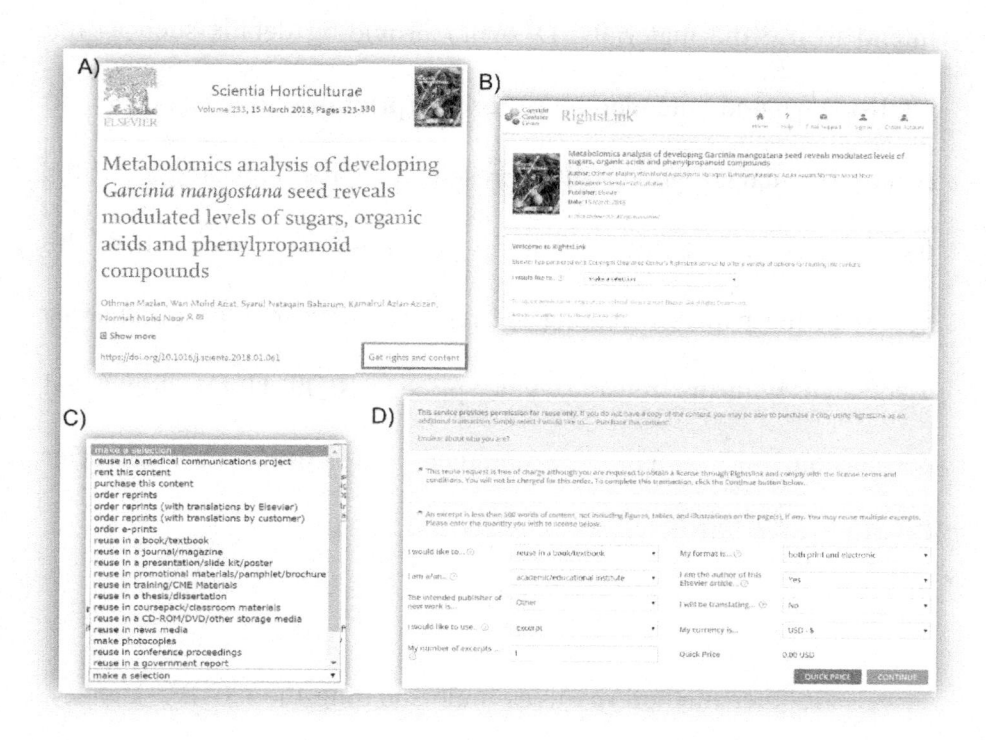

Figure 7.11 Obtaining permission for the use of journal materials through a publisher's website involves the following steps: A) Any journal publication website will typically have a section labeled "Get rights and content" or a similar indication for their published manuscripts (highlighted in red). B) Upon selecting this option, authors will be redirected to RightsLink, where they can officially request permission for reuse. C) Authors can then specify how they

intend to use the materials. D) After providing details such as the publisher's name, intended reuse format (print or online or both), and other particulars, a price will be presented for the requested use. This fee must be paid before obtaining permission. In cases where the author of the paper is making the request, there may be no charges associated with its reuse (Quick price = 0.00 USD). Reprinted permission was obtained from Elsevier (https://doi.org/10.1016/j.scienta.2018.01.061).

Another method involves understanding the CC-BY legality, where certain materials can be freely copied and modified, as outlined in Table 7.1. For example, if a copyrighted material is classified under CC BY NC ND, its reuse must adhere to Creative Commons licensing (CC), credit the original owner (BY), refrain from commercial gain (NC), and avoid any modifications (ND). In the case of CC BY SA, the material can be used for commercial purposes but still within the framework of CC licensing, requiring proper citation while maintaining the original license type. Various combinations of these licensing types, as elaborated in Table 7.1, may exist, and authors should be cognizant of such restrictions.

Table 7.1 Different copyright license types are identified by specific abbreviations, symbols, and meanings.

Copyright license types	Abbrev.	Symbols	Meaning
Creative Commons	CC	(cc)	The material is covered by a Creative Commons License, permitting copying, distribution, and usage, subject to other applicable copyright types.
Attribution	BY	(person symbol)	Any reproduction, distribution, and

			utilization must be attributed to the owner of the materials.
No Derivatives	ND	⊜	No alterations or modifications to the original material are permitted.
No Commercial	NC	🚫$	The utilization of the material should not be of a commercial nature.
Share Alike	SA	↻	Users must retain similar license types when utilizing the material.

Alternatively, copyright reuse approval can be obtained through communication with the copyright holder via email. It is essential to bear in mind that legal consequences may ensue if materials are utilized without proper authorization. Therefore, seeking explicit permission is imperative before incorporating any content into publications or written productions. In some instances, original authors may generously permit reuse without imposing charges. Alternatively, negotiations can be initiated to establish terms and conditions for the usage of the materials.

Fabrication

Another pitfall in scientific writing is fabrication (Figure 7.12). Fabrication involves the deceptive manipulation or cherry-picking of data to selectively bolster or refute an argument. This unethical act carries severe consequences and may lead to expulsion from a research institution. Furthermore, individuals engaging in such misconduct often face ridicule from the scientific community, potentially hindering their ability to pursue a future career in science.

Figure 7.12 Another pitfall in scientific writing is data fabrication—presenting falsified data to support a specific hypothesis or argument.

Permission to reuse the figure has been obtained from Glasbergen Cartoon Service (http://www.glasbergen.com).

Regrettably, there have been several documented cases of papers being retracted due to data fabrication. For instance, a study on carcinoma was retracted by the journal "Aging" in 2020 owing to falsified and fabricated data (https://doi.org/10.18632/aging.205525) (Figure 7.13). Previously in 2006, a South Korean scientist was accused of fabricating data concerning stem cell research, which had been published in the Science journal (https://www.science.org/doi/10.1126/science.1094515). Following an investigation conducted by Seoul National University, the manuscript was retracted. A website known as Retraction Watch maintains an expanding catalogue of retracted articles (https://retractionwatch.com/). These retracted papers remain accessible online, albeit labelled with a "Retracted" designation. This unfortunately confers a lasting stigma upon both the paper and its authors, extending beyond the primary contributors. Even collaborators, who may not have participated in the specific experiment conducted by the principal author, bear responsibility and cannot disassociate themselves from the authorship list. This highlights the significance of the ICJME guideline mentioned earlier, wherein assuming authorship entails accepting all associated responsibilities. Consequently, all individuals involved will face implications.

Figure 7.13 The ramifications of data fabrication can have severe consequences for scientists. The left panel displays the manuscript

with a retraction label (https://doi.org/10.18632/aging.102756). On the right panel, a corresponding note accompanies the retracted article, providing justification for the retraction, in this instance attributed to data fabrication (https://doi.org/10.18632/aging.205525). Reprinted with permission under the Creative Commons Attribution 3.0 and 4.0 CC-BY licenses, respectively.

Predatory publication

A relatively recent ethical concern involves the publication in predatory journals. This term applies to specific journals that primarily target paid authors, whose articles may be accepted without the rigorous scrutiny of the peer-review process. Many of these journals engage in direct email outreach to authors, encouraging publication in their journals, as exemplified in this instance (Figure 7.14).

> Good Morning!
> Can we have your article for successful release of our Upcoming Issue.
> Well, we would like to release the **upcoming Issue** of our ▓▓▓▓▓▓▓▓▓▓▓▓▓▓▓ -1241) on 25ᵗʰ **October.**
> Since we in short of **one article** towards successful release of our next issue, we need your intervention by **any type of article** to accomplish this issue.
> I hope **2 pages article** isn't time taken for eminent author like you.
> Await your promising response.
> Best Regards,

Figure 7.14 A deceptive email soliciting manuscripts for publication in a journal might tempt scientists with the promise of quick and easy publishing. It is important to be aware that such journals could be predatory, driven solely by profit and lacking genuine interest in your scientific work!

In scholarly circles, journals indexed by Web of Science (administered by Clarivate Analytics) and Scopus (administered by Scimago) are generally regarded as reputable publications (Figure 7.15). To ascertain the status of your preferred journal, you can verify its listing on both Scopus (https://www.scimagojr.com/journalrank.php) and Web of Science (https://incites.thomsonreuters.com/) using your institutional account (access to these websites is typically restricted to on-campus or research institution locations that subscribe to these services).

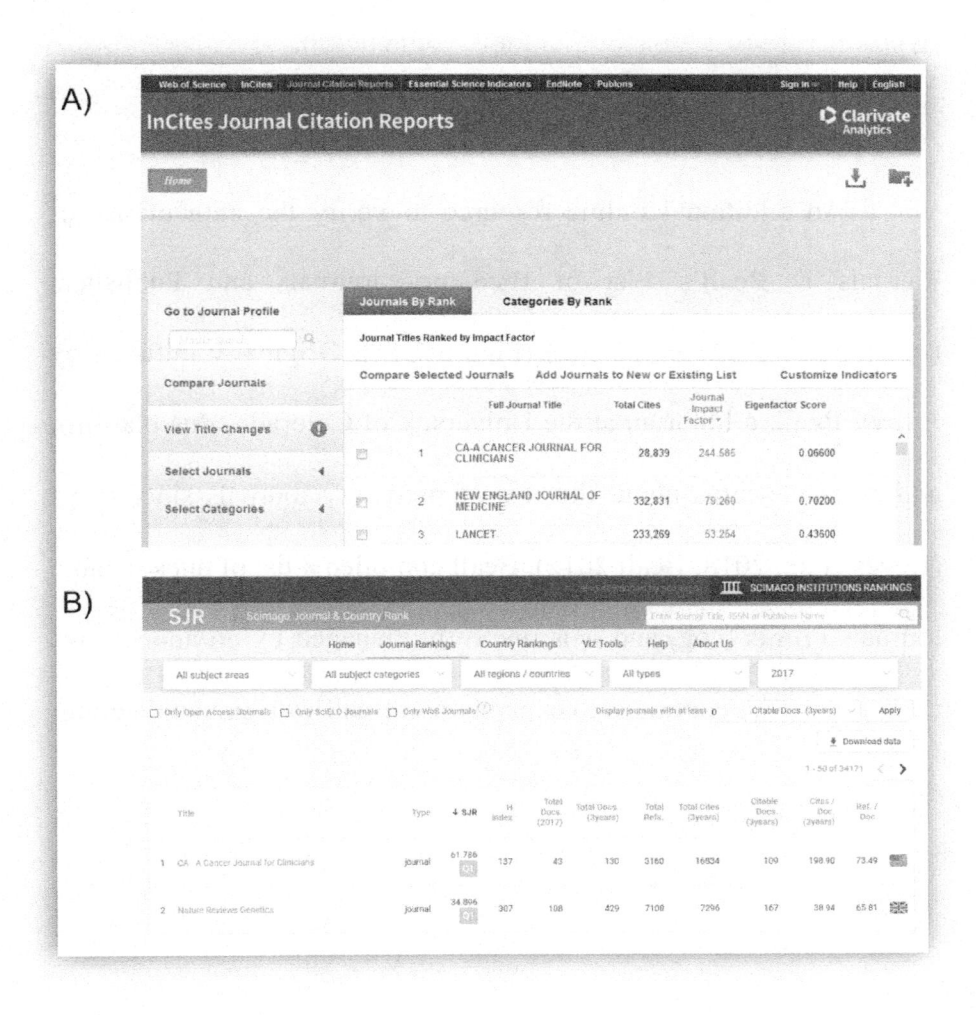

A) [Screenshot of InCites Journal Citation Reports homepage showing journals ranked by Impact Factor: 1. CA-A Cancer Journal for Clinicians (28,839 total cites; 244.585 impact factor; 0.06600 Eigenfactor Score); 2. New England Journal of Medicine (332,831; 79.260; 0.70200); 3. Lancet (233,269; 53.254; 0.43600).]

B) [Screenshot of SCImago Journal & Country Rank (SJR) website showing journals ranked by SJR: 1. CA - A Cancer Journal for Clinicians (SJR 61.786; H index 137; Total Docs (2017) 43; Total Docs (3years) 130; Total Refs. 3160; Total Cites (3years) 16934; Citable Docs (3years) 109; Cites/Doc (2years) 198.90; Ref./Doc 73.49); 2. Nature Reviews Genetics (SJR 34.806; H index 307; 108; 429; 7108; 7296; 167; 38.94; 65.81).]

Figure 7.15 The webpages for checking journals indexed by both Web of Science (A) (https://jcr.clarivate.com/JCRJournalHomeAction.action) and Scopus (B) (https://www.scimagojr.com/journalrank.php).

An additional online resource to verify the authenticity of journals is Beall's List of Predatory Journals and Publishers (https://beallslist.weebly.com/) (Figure 7.16). Originally initiated by Jeffrey Beall, a librarian at the University of Colorado, this platform addresses concerns about the rise of predatory journals since 2012 (Revés et al., 2018; Beall 2012). Beall compiled a list of questionable journals on his blog, and it is presently managed by an anonymous contributor who continues to expand upon Beall's original collection.

Figure 7.16 The homepage of Beall's List of Predatory Journals and Publishers can be accessed at https://beallslist.weebly.com/.

Chapter 8 How to mitigate problems in writing?

Find help

We have previously acknowledged that the publication journey can be a prolonged and challenging process fraught with ethical considerations. Nevertheless, potential conflicts or challenges may arise at various stages, spanning from the initial writing phase to the point of publication. The most effective approach is to engage in direct communication with your supervisor, seeking clarity on any emerging issues (Figure 8.1). If this avenue proves insufficient, it is advisable to approach and discuss the matter with co-supervisors. Additionally, seeking assistance from friends and colleagues can provide valuable insights to address potential problems encountered along the way.

If conflict happens?

Talk directly to your supervisor- be clear → Talk to your co-supervisor → Talk to your friends → Get help from institutional counselor

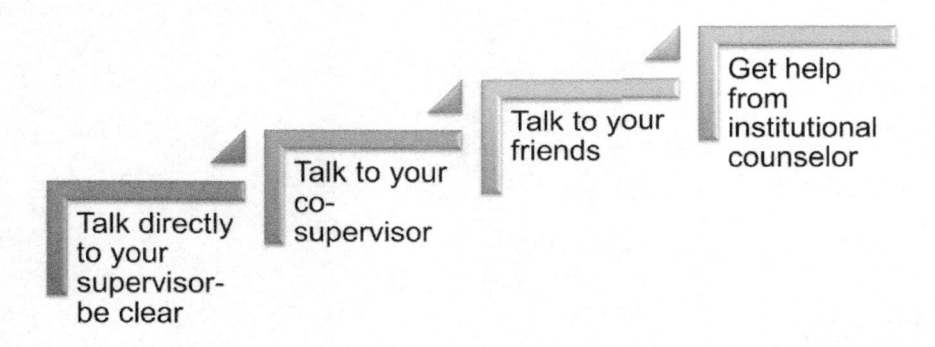

Figure 8.1 Several options are available for seeking help in the event of conflicts during studentship.

In more serious cases, it is crucial for students to seek assistance from institutional counselors. Students may be susceptible to mental health challenges such as depression and anxiety. Rather than allowing these issues to accumulate, it is imperative to address them as promptly as possible. The support of a counselor can alleviate, or at least mitigate, the cumulative burden of emotional struggles.

Students, particularly those engaged in research, should be aware that challenges with supervision are not isolated occurrences and should be approached with compassion and open discussion. However, serious issues in writing rarely arise unless the supervisor is genuinely uncooperative in assisting students in completing their manuscripts. Most, if not all, supervisors are scientists, making publication a top priority. In many instances, supervisors may be tardy in returning drafts, hence students should also have the capacity to 'manage' their supervisors, as discussed in Chapter 3.

Social network and online pages

An additional strategy to navigate challenges in research involves tapping into your social network. It is essential, however, to strike a balance and avoid excessive time spent on social media, ensuring it does not interfere with your primary research responsibilities. Injecting an element of enjoyment into your research is encouraged.

Numerous social media pages, such as the Doctorate/PhD Support Group (Figure 8.2), actively support research students by sharing valuable information on scientific knowledge and breakthroughs. Engaging with these platforms can enhance your overall understanding of science and potentially contribute to your individual research endeavors.

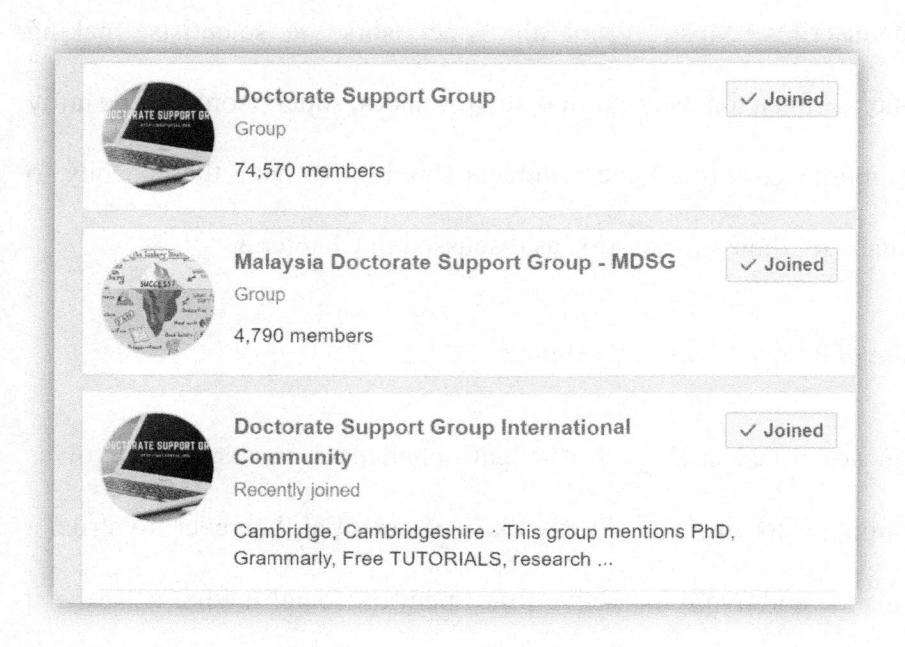

	Doctorate Support Group Group 74,570 members	✓ Joined
	Malaysia Doctorate Support Group - MDSG Group 4,790 members	✓ Joined
	Doctorate Support Group International Community Recently joined Cambridge, Cambridgeshire · This group mentions PhD, Grammarly, Free TUTORIALS, research ...	✓ Joined

Figure 8.2 Several social media pages provide support for postgraduate students. These platforms offer advice, tips, and motivation throughout our research journey.

Other online platforms, albeit less scientific and informal, can also be valuable for providing memes and jokes related to research. One notable example is PhD (Pile Higher and Deeper) comics (http://phdcomics.com/) (Figure 8.3). This platform humorously portrays the lives of scientists and research students. Such comedic relief can prove beneficial during stressful moments in the research journey, perhaps after facing paper rejection. After all, laughter is the best medicine.

Figure 8.3 The "Piled Higher and Deeper" webcomic (www.phdcomics.com) serves as a means of escape from the stresses encountered in laboratories. Created by Jorge Cham, it provides a lighthearted perspective on the challenges faced by individuals involved in academic and research pursuits.

Conclusion

In conclusion, it is evident that both students and supervisors play pivotal roles in ensuring the success of any publication, especially in papers involving multiple authors where meeting all comments can pose a challenge. Crucially, the experimental design should be determined early on, ideally before commencing any laboratory work. This foresight can significantly mitigate hassles and headaches during the writing process. One key aspect of successful collaboration with your supervisor is to finalize figures and tables even before drafting the manuscript. These visual elements are the outcomes of a well-considered experimental design and contribute to the strength of the paper. Throughout the writing process, effective and clear communication is paramount. Approach your writing as if you were a potential reader of the paper, ensuring clarity and coherence. Additionally, always uphold ethical standards in every aspect and situation. The repercussions of ethical misconduct can be severe, potentially jeopardizing one's career. Hence, it is imperative to avoid such misconduct at all costs. Lastly, writing is not without its challenges, whether in the preparation stages or during the reviewing process. In times of turbulence, seek assistance from various sources. Remember, "no man is an island," and collective efforts should be made to resolve any issues encountered during the paper's writing. Ultimately, successful writing starts with YOU!

References

Ahmad, R., Sahidin, I., Taher, M., Low, C., Noor, N.M., Sillapachaiyaporn, C., Chuchawankul, S., Sarachana, T., Tencomnao, T., Iskandar, F. and Rajab, N.F., 2018. Polygonumins A, a newly isolated compound from the stem of *Polygonum minus* Huds with potential medicinal activities. Scientific Reports, 8(1), 4202.

Aizat, W.M., Ahmad-Hashim, F.H. and Jaafar, S.N.S., 2019. Valorization of mangosteen, "The Queen of Fruits," and new advances in postharvest and in food and engineering applications: A review. Journal of Advanced Research, 20, 61-70.

Aslaksen, H. and Sletsjøe, A.B., 2009. Generators of matrix algebras in dimension 2 and 3. Linear Algebra and its Applications, 430(1), 1-6.

Beall, J., 2012. Predatory publishers are corrupting open access. Nature News, 489(7415), 179.

Bornmann, L. and Daniel, H.D., 2010. How long is the peer review process for journal manuscripts? A case study on Angewandte Chemie International Edition. CHIMIA International Journal for Chemistry, 64(1), 72-77.

Bunawan, H., Talip, N. and Noor, N.M., 2011. Foliar anatomy and micromorphology of *Polygonum minus* (Huds) and their taxonomic implications. Australian Journal of Crop Science, 5(2), 123.

Cargill, M. and O'Connor, P., 2013. Writing scientific research articles: Strategy and steps. John Wiley & Sons.

Damanhoury, S., Newton, A.S., Rashid, M., Hartling, L., Byrne, J.L.S. and Ball, G.D.C., 2018. Defining metabolically healthy obesity in children: a scoping review. Obesity reviews, 19(11), 1476-1491.

Lacombe, J., Armstrong, M.E., Wright, F.L. and Foster, C., 2019. The impact of physical activity and an additional behavioural risk factor on cardiovascular disease, cancer and all-cause mortality: a systematic review. BMC Public Health, 19(900), 1-16.

Lee, X.W., Mat-Isa, M.N., Mohd-Elias, N.A., Aizat-Juhari, M.A., Goh, H.H., Dear, P.H., Chow, K.S., Adam, J.H., Mohamed, R., Firdaus-Raih, M. and Wan, K.L., 2016. Perigone lobe transcriptome analysis provides insights into Rafflesia cantleyi flower development. PloS One, 11(12), e0167958.

Li, J.X., Fan, L.C., Li, M.H., Cao, W.J. and Xu, J.F., 2017. Beneficial effects of Omalizumab therapy in allergic bronchopulmonary aspergillosis: a synthesis review of published literature. Respiratory Medicine, 122, 33-42.

Moher, D., Liberati, A., Tetzlaff, J. and Altman, D.G., 2009. Preferred reporting items for systematic reviews and meta-analyses: the PRISMA statement. Annals of Internal Medicine, 151(4), 264-269.

Munn, Z., Peters, M.D., Stern, C., Tufanaru, C., McArthur, A. and Aromataris, E., 2018. Systematic review or scoping review? Guidance for authors when choosing between a systematic or scoping review approach. BMC Medical Research Methodology, 18(1), p.143.

Pang, S.L., Ho, K.L., Waterman, J., Rambo, R.P., Teh, A.H., Mathavan, I., Harris, G., Beis, K., Say, Y.H., Anusha, M.S. and Sio, Y.Y., 2019. Crystal structure and epitope analysis of house dust mite allergen Der f 21. Scientific Reports, 9(1), 4933.

Pham, M.T., Rajić, A., Greig, J.D., Sargeant, J.M., Papadopoulos, A. and McEwen, S.A., 2014. A scoping review of scoping reviews: advancing the approach and enhancing the consistency. Research Synthesis Methods, 5(4), 371-385.

Revés, J., da Silva, B.M., Durão, J., Ribeiro, N.V., Lemos, S. and Escada, P., 2018. Predatory publishing: an industry that is threatening science. Acta Medica Portuguesa, 31(3), 141-143.

SCIENTIFIC ARTICLE WRITING (SAW) 101

Index

A

authors · 52, 145, 229
authorship · 184, 194

C

citation · 55, 138
Copyright · 201, 205

E

Ethics · 182
experiments · 55, 58

F

fabrication · 207

H

history · 38

J

journal · 109, 133, 227

L

laboratory · 58
language · 55, 62, 145

P

postgraduate · 50
publication · 54, 145, 187, 211

R

review
  peer · 38, 41, 104, 137, 138, 141, 142, 143, 144, 146, 151, 153, 157, 227, 228, 229

S

student · 58
submission · 95
supervisor · 50, 58, 68

T

teacher · 50

W

writing
  scientific · 48, 51, 55, 58, 62, 68, 143, 217

About the Author

Dr. Wan Mohd Aizat earned his Bachelor's degree (Hons.) and PhD from The University of Adelaide, Australia, with specializations in Biotechnology and Plant Science. He currently holds a position as a research fellow and senior lecturer at the Institute of Systems Biology (INBIOSIS), Universiti Kebangsaan Malaysia (UKM). With a prolific academic career, he has authored and co-authored cumulatively over 70 peer-reviewed articles, scientific books and chapters in books. Dr. Wan Mohd Aizat actively engages in nurturing students' writing skills, providing guidance in manuscript preparation and enhancing their language proficiency. His dedication extends to organizing classes and seminars on student academic development, covering topics such as "Writing with Your Supervisor," "Endnote Practical Course," and "Systematic Review Techniques—Incorporating Web of Science, Scopus, and other Databases." Dr. Wan Mohd Aizat's primary interest lies in fostering strong and trusting relationships between students and supervisors, recognizing their pivotal role in achieving successful scientific publications.

Made in the USA
Columbia, SC
21 May 2024